Instinct

Instinct

(Roman Ruminations, Volume Two)

by
Norman Weeks

"Urge and urge and urge,
Always the procreant urge of the world."
—— Walt Whitman

From Primordial Cell to Psychoanalysis

[Readers: Pack your mind for a long, long trip.]

165

Loneliness is an affliction of the human as a conscious self. Also of the human is instinct. Instinct, the animal energetic to mate and bond and procreate, has not been left behind by the *enculturated animal.* And so, instinct is a problem for the human. It too may become an affliction.

My own loneliness at leisure in Rome presents an opportunity to get a lot of reading done. I have availed myself of that opportunity.

I read all the books, yet I still didn't understand anything of human psychology. The bibliographies of the academics and clinicians feed off one another; it all seemed to me mere rearrangements of words, verbiage upon verbiage, concepts and constructs, a semantic game. Where in all that conceptualizing was the entire real-life human, that creature of loneliness and instinct and love?

We might as well throw out all the modern literature and return to the insights of the ancient myths, I concluded. The professor in his chair doesn't know half of what the old storyteller by the fire knew. Every myth is an aperture to the human mind.

Having become disillusioned with the literature, I had the happy inspiration to seek out human psychology in works of art. There was more to be found in the museums of Rome, I suspected, than just an inventory of aesthetic images. Art is out of the unconscious. Could I interpret its revelation?

Here was a fascinating and challenging task,— to read the human mind in the form of the human body, the pagan idol, to draw out the living dynamic from inert stone. The classical sculpture of the museums of Rome depicts the fireside myths. It is, then, the very *embodi*ment of insight regarding human nature. Ancient sculpture may contain some secrets that no modern psychologist has yet deciphered.

Into the museums and galleries, then. The mute statuary might tell me what I want to know. If we become idolaters once again, we may gain entrance into the penetralia of the human soul.

The idol is the oracle.

166

During one of my habitual Sunday morning visits to the Capitoline Museums, I discovered that a wing that had long been closed for restoration and rearrangement was open again. I immediately entered the corridor to search for a small bronze statue, the Alexandrine Hermaphrodite, which I had seen once and which has been on my mind since.

I found it in the same corner, amidst the general rearrangement, but it was larger than I remembered it, about thirty-two inches tall with the base. It is inconspicuous, because it is now surrounded by various dismembered colossal fragments,—a hind-half of a bull, a horse, and a huge head and hand of Constans II. All are now in a room designated the Sala dei Bronzi; the only thing the pieces in the heterogeneous assemblage have in common is the metal material of their composition.

Hermaphroditos, the mythmaker said, was the son of the god Hermes and the goddess Aphrodite. An incarnation of double-divine physical beauty in the flesh, Hermaphroditos was loved by Salmakis, a fountain nymph. When he resisted and rebuffed her, Salmakis prayed to the gods to unite her forever with Hermaphroditos. The gods granted her plea, fusing the two of them into a single person, now Hermaphrodite, the actual embodiment of male and female become inseparably one.

The Alexandrine Hermaphrodite is a standing bronze nude of beautiful form and dual sex and gender, with a classic male/female head, phallus erect, moderate perfect breasts, and arms outstretched, reaching for the viewer in soft feminine acceptance.

I oscillated slowly in an arc in front of the figure. From each position the face seemed to shift subtly along the gender spectrum, now masculine, now feminine, now indeterminate. Similarly, the sensuality of the flesh—the skin and muscles and limbs—appeared male or female or both as I scanned and blinked. Transfixed by the idol, in simple receptivity, I felt hushed in awe at the idea, if not at this particular execution of it.

I studied and stared at the Alexandrine Hermaphrodite for a long time, both as a work of art and as a psychological clue. I reacted with the same responsiveness I had felt when I first discovered it. An appreciator of either sex must feel drawn to that body with a human erotic desire. One identifies with the sameness, one is drawn to the complementarity, in that embodied representation of complete human sexuality. There is a love-triangle of Narcissus, Eros, and Hermaphrodite,—of self-love, otherness love, and total love.

The Alexandrine Hermaphrodite of the Capitoline Museums is so small compared to the other bronzes in the gallery and in such a secluded nook that most visitors pass it by without really seeing it. Those who stopped to look did so with only a cursory glance, in uncomprehending distraction. Most museum-goers are mere label readers, as if mere identification were appreciation and understanding. A few visitors, just come from church, when they drew close to look, did see, and they quickly retreated in Christian revulsion, as if their cultivated Sunday morning piety had just been spoiled.

But there is a mystery to be reverenced here, not a theological one, idol though this is. There is a human psychological mystery here.

167

When Nathaniel Hawthorne was in Rome, he chanced to visit a fellow American who was a sculptor, resident here to draw inspiration from the classical artifacts.

Hawthorne found him in his studio, carving away at a colossal nude hero in the idolatrous style of the ancient pagans. Hawthorne found the very idea absurd. Remarking to his notebook, if not to the sculptor, Hawthorne said that we are so clothed, body and mind, birth-to-death, that an artist has no more right to depict a man naked than he does to depict him flayed.

Yes, we have left behind paganism, the naughty childhood of our race, and put on clothing as a dermic identity. In his disapproval of the sculptor's project, Hawthorne was not so much the prudish New England Puritan as an honest psychologist. Naked no more, this modern human being. We see ourselves, and so should portray ourselves, as the clothed animal.

However, there was plenty of nakedness in ancient Rome, as I realize when I walk through the capacious halls of the Baths of Caracalla or the Baths of Diocletian. Mediterranean nakedness extended even to the communal privies, with their dozen holes side by side, so strange to our modern sense of physiological privacy.

We can't be naked anymore, because of Christianity, which joined the adjectives *naked* and *ashamed* in an indissoluble molten link. We can no longer be naked innocently or look at a nude innocently. Actual nakedness is temptation leading to the sin of lust, nakedness in art verges into pornography. There is a cultural taboo upon *full frontal nudity*, whether of the living body or of any representation of a living body, say in movies. In abhorrence of the pagan classical aesthetic, the heavy negative moral judgment of Christianity indicts the nude.

Christian religion, the soul at war with the body, made the natural forbidden, only to make us crave the natural all the more. Isn't there now something perverse in our nostalgia for nakedness? The desire to see nakedness, voyeurism, is a neurosis of the clothed and sickly ones.

Living in Rome as I do, I might think that the righteous Christian taboo upon nakedness has been left behind. Even the popes, after all, filled their celibate cloister of the Vatican with promiscuous nudes, ancient or contemporary, the works of Michelangelo the most outrageous affront to the taboo. But I think the pagan nostalgia of the Renaissance popes was as psychologically absurd as that of our nineteenth-century expatriate American sculptor.

The body is a physical fact, the soul a metaphysical fantasy. Christian scruples have put a fig leaf upon the body. Who is now healthy enough to look upon the nude in a wholesome spirit? Could there be such a son-of-Nature, immune to his own upbringing and to the chronic pathology of our religious inheritance?

We might as well pack off the nude statues of Rome to the niches of the catacombs, inter them there behind sepulchral slabs until some cultural resurrection-of-the-dead.

There can be no return to Eden before the Fall or to pagan idyll, however pressing may be our nostalgia. The many classical nudes in the museums of Rome are like postcards from paradise. "A wonderful time....Wish you were here."

Our aesthetics regarding classical nudes is a wanderlust. Although absurd and nostalgic, it seeks human self-understanding and the satisfaction of human longing.

168

Pursuing my quest for instinct among the sculpture galleries of Rome, I paid a visit to the National Roman Museum, a great repository of classical art located in the Baths of Diocletian, just a few minutes' walk from my *pensione.*

There I came upon the Sleeping Hermaphrodite, a near-life-size marble sculpture of a prone recumbent nude, a Hellenistic work of about 160 B.C. There is another copy of the lost original in the Borghese Gallery here in Rome and still others in the Uffizi in Florence and in the Louvre.

My approach was interrupted by a foreign school group passing through. The teacher, stereotypically British, hurried his students past the Sleeping Hermaphrodite with apparent proper embarrassment. He spat out the epithet *Bisexual!* at it, as if Hermaphrodite were a freak-of-Nature, a monster, or a pathological medical curiosity. He displayed the revulsion one might feel upon unexpectedly encountering a paraplegic in a beauty contest.

Was that all that he, a teacher of art, could make of what Pliny described as "the noble Hermaphrodite"? I began to suspect that we moderns, when we look at classical antiquity through the dark tinted, nearly opaque lenses of Christianity, are mostly blind to the simple beauty and mystic meaning of ancient art. The animality that was the wellspring of the pagan mind belongs to an earlier, a more natural, state than the wearied cerebralism of us moderns.

The Sleeping Hermaphrodite was summarily dismissed by the academic, but that did not discourage me from closer scrutiny. After the school group left with a flurry and a few snickers, I approached the statue and circled it slowly.

The body of the Sleeping Hermaphrodite is rendered as duosexual, that imagery so disconcerting to our modern scruple. The work is an attempt to create a composite of biological beauty and the all of the sexuality of the human into a single body.

169

A perverse idea, according to the Christians. A bizarre freak and monster, according to the academics. Most of the critical judgments upon Hermaphrodite have been negative.

Like the teacher I encountered in the museum, the scholars have treated Hermaphrodite from a perspective of pathology. What little literature there is on the subject generally casts a psychiatric eye upon Hermaphrodite.

Artistic representations of Hermaphrodite are relegated to the catalog of decadent grotesqueries. A quote from an academic as example: "The subjects of Hellenistic art range from infancy to decrepitude, from divinity to depravity; not content with two sexes, they imagine intermediate beings, hermaphrodites."

"Not content with two sexes"? Right there the academic stumbled upon the psychological truth, only to flee from it in revulsion. Hermaphrodite is no "intermediate being", a half-and-half. Hermaphrodite is a synthesis; it is completeness.

According to the academics, the myth and art of Hermaphrodite belong to the realm of aberration: "From the fourth century B.C. onwards, when the taste of Greek sculptors was beginning to degenerate, this ambiguous figure was in high favor, and numerous representations, many having a morbid beauty, survive."

"Morbid beauty"! Would the academic art critics use that phrase to describe the iconography of the Crucifixion?

Anyway, the modern supercivilized mind perceives Hermaphrodite in the contexts of depravity, decadence, and degeneracy.

If Hermaphrodite is merely a bizarre specimen of physical and psychological abnormality, then even the sleep of the Sleeping Hermaphrodite is perverse. The statue is described as "a spirally contorted Sleeping Hermaphrodite in the throes of an erotic dream". The critics do not hesitate to penetrate into the mind of the marble. They detect "uneasy sleep disturbed by nervousness and expectation of love". So, Hermaphrodite sleeps an agitated sleep, or not sleep at all, but really nightmare, the nightmare of perverse sexuality erupted into grotesque art.

Academics less censorious have tried to interpret Hermaphrodite as an *etiological myth*, that is, an attempt to account for the birth of actual physical hermaphrodites. I doubt that. The birth of true hermaphrodites is an occurrence so rare that few people would have witnessed it and demanded an explanation, one that would come to include not only the myth, but abundant artworks as well. The etiological interpretation, attempting to explain away, doesn't explain at all.

170

The academics pass judgment, they themselves incapable of creating anything. What about the creative geniuses, the artists of deep imagination, those who might possess the insight that would lead to perceptive wisdom?

What would D.H. Lawrence, our modern advocate of instinct, have to say about the problem of Hermaphrodite?

In his mystical rhapsody, *Fantasia of the Unconscious*, Lawrence dismissed what he called "the hermaphrodite fallacy". Yet I think that Hermaphrodite is no more a fallacy than the X-Y chromosomes in my own body.

Lawrence was disturbed by the muddling of sexual polarity due to shifting social roles in his

[16]

society. Either/or polarity must be the norm of sexual health, he insisted.

D.H. Lawrence was a polemicist inveighing a-gainst the depolarizing of sexual relationships that he detected in his society. But Hermaphrodite is not to be interpreted in terms of British social pathology. There is a muddling of gender distinction aplenty in our modern world, but nowhere have I ever met a single devotee of Hermaphrodite.

171

Why do I feel an attraction toward an image that stirs up such revulsion in others?

I looked upon the Sleeping Hermaphrodite. There is, true, a restlessness in the figure. Hermaphrodite struggles against the blanket over his/her nakedness, that smothering cover of clothed civilizedness. Deep in sleep, Hermaphrodite kicks away the blanket with the right foot, pulls away from it with the left leg, turns the head away, as the coils of the covering twist around the left arm like a fetter. The image portrays the resistance of the organic animal to the confines of civilized restraint. Hermaphrodite is attempting to uncover and expose a mystery.

The statue reveals the Hellenistic interest in unconsciousness, or, as we would say in modern terms, *the unconscious*. Reminiscent of the sleeping or drunken satyrs, sleeping *Erotes* and children, the Sleeping Ariadne, Endymion, and the dying Persians, Gauls, and Amazons exhibited in the museums of Rome, the Sleeping Hermaphrodite seems to the contemplative observer to say as much about sleep and death as about life and sex.

The image of Hermaphrodite belongs not to the underworld of pornography, but to the horizons of psychology. Any salacious interest is dissuaded by Hermaphrodite's eyes, closed in the utter innocence of sleep. Hermaphrodite, lax in the unconsciousness of sleep, breathes that spirit of ambiguous androgyny that we see in the bodies of children.

172

Androgyny; male/female. (*Andró-gynous* in the Greek.) Isn't there a recurrent ambiguity of gender in the Mediterranean pagan representations of ideal human beauty? The head and face of Apollo, especially, are often sculpted with a delicacy and refinement that make that ideal male appear fair and feminine. Correspondingly, Athena (as warrior) and Artemis (as hunter) have their masculine traits.

In classical art, human physical beauty tends toward androgyny. From the feminization of Apollo and the masculinization of Athena and Artemis to the unification of opposite sexes in Hermaphrodite there is a single, albeit spectacular, step of artistic imagination.

In Hermaphrodite, the artist composed (put together) and comprehended (held together) the split halfness of the human being into a wholeness. Hermaphrodite, then, is a culmination of the development of an androgynous aesthetic.

If so, a complete change of interpretive perspective becomes necessary,—away from physical hermaphroditism, toward psychical androgyny. Hermaphrodite sleeps. And sleeping within all of us, deep in our unconscious, is an androgyny.

173

The sexes are strange to each other. No wonder, because each one of us is strange to ourself. What is more strange than existence, individuality, consciousness, life?

An early awareness is, "Here I am." Then comes "What am I?"

The obvious answer to the "What am I?" is the body. We discover our body as the vessel of life and awareness.

We come to the experience of others as the experience of the bodies of others. There are bodies like our own,—the same sex, and bodies different from our own,—the other sex. And yet, there is a commonality and warm sympathy between all the bodies. Humanness has two body forms, but it is the same humanness.

A later question might be, "Why am I this body, male and not that body, female?" or vice versa. The otherness of the other sex is a puzzle.

Then, hormones arouse instinct. The adolescent discovers within a powerful craving for the other sex. Does the other feel the same need I do? Do I understand the other sex? How to approach? The otherness is not only anatomical and genital difference, but something in the psychology of the other sex.

Even in that psychology there is, once again, a commonality along with the difference. The sexes may experience feelings differently and may perceive and think differently, but they are both human, humans who need each other. Instinct provokes that need.

Differences there are, but it is not a simple either/or between the sexes. There is overlap in characteristics, the one somehow also in the other. The sexes, after all, are not different species, but only differentiation within a single species. Sharing the same origin, the two sexes commingle in a common human nature.

Despite difficulties in mutual understanding, communicating, relating—the puzzle of the otherness—, the two sexes are in a profound sense one kind.

Nonetheless, each feels split off from the other, each craves bonding, union with the other... Or might it be re-union?

Why are there the two different sexes? Why do the two sexes crave to be united into one? It's not only a necessity for reproduction, not just a physical drive, but an existential longing. Hermaphrodite is a portrayal of that longing.

174

I was dissatisfied with D.H. Lawrence's summary dismissal of "the hermaphrodite fallacy" and his equating of androgyny with homosexuality. What about our other modern exegete of sex, Sigmund Freud. What did he think about the problem of androgyny?

In the murkiest and most profound of his later books, Freud speculated that antecedent to maleness and femaleness was a *primordial cell*, the single, self-fertilizing source of generation, the prototype from which every living being descended.

How similar that hypothesis is to some myths of wise primitives. The modern mind of our pre-eminent psychologist plagiarizes the ancients once again. (Freud himself was, in fact, a mythologist; his characters were not personages, but psychical entities conflicting with one another in dramatic situations of the mind.)

If the two sexes actually came about as a schism from some primordial unity, then androgyny, far from being a late decadence, is really a reversion to the wholeness of origin.

Androgyny as a fusion of opposites may exist, then, at a deep unconscious level that hearkens back to the original splitting-off of the two sexes out of the antecedent primordial cell. Freud provided more insight into Hermaphrodite and the problem of psychical androgyny than Lawrence did.

Before there even was sex, there was the primordial cell. That cell engendered all life. The male megalomaniacal myth of Genesis must be rejected as just patriarchal propaganda against the female. No male God removed woman from the side of man, from some phallic rib. Rather, the primordial eve-cell gave birth to an adam-cell, then later took him back into herself to generate new forms of life from combination.

The split into two sexes came about by evolution out of the single primordial cell. The asexual reproduction and parthenogenesis still to be found in Nature are vestiges and evidence of the origin of all life.

175

Given sufficient resources in the environment, the primordial cell, the perfect sphere, might have replicated sameness indefinitely. It could have reproduced new identical cells over and over again out of its own self-renewing energy, like that of Life Itself. With that total self-sufficiency, the primordial cell could have been the only form of life in perpetuity,—but only as cloning may be a perpetual process.

However, when the primordial cell split off a new cell as the agent of future reproduction, the initiative was to prove momentous. For the new cell—now let's call it the male— was defective, as Y is of X. When the male linked up with the primordial cell, now the female, at the same time that it inseminated her with new, varied life, it impregnated her with a now hereditary defect.

The first act of coitus, at some auroral hour of evolution, determined our fate. Thus did mortality enter into the world. Genesis misrepresents the origin of death, as it does the origin of life. Our mortality is not to be explained by the Original Sin (a sin, incidentally, blamed upon the female), but, rather, by the defective nature of the male and its pathogenic infection of the female.

Even if taken as sin, the male's deed was not culpable, because it was inadvertent, due to an unperceived defect. Nor can the female be blamed for her act of generation of variety by means of re-acceptance of her own created life back into herself. There is nothing moral about immortality, nothing immoral about mortality. The intrusion of death into the generation of life was an evolutionary accident.

In every coitus of cells since the first one, when the ovum-sphere is penetrated by the sperm-vector, life gets contaminated with mortality. Our end was predetermined by our beginning.

176

We are uncountable evolutionary generations away from the very first coitus of cells. Yet, instinct compels each of us to repeat, not the Original Sin, but the original act. Human coitus is a re-enactment of the primal event of the evolution of Life. The male, through his extension, returns to the source of life, that he may enable the female to continue giving birth to new life. Not merely the "procreant urge" (a physical and hormonal drive), instinct is also a powerful existential imperative to re-immerse oneself back into oneness, as in the oneness of the primordial cell.

Instinct as drive is a problem for human self-estimate. No matter our pretensions to a mind and soul that transcend mere Nature, instinct is what moves us still. Instinct is the dynamic of Life Itself, in the enculturated human animal as fully as in the so-called lower creatures.

Our problem with instinct is the human's metaphysical self-estimate and a willfulness to act up to it. Self-directedness and self-control grapple with instinct. The human wants to subdue instinct and subject it to control.

The human has found instinct a formidable force within. We may be conscious of what it is that we are doing, we may resist it, we may judge it, we may even despise it, but do it we must. Instinct presses irresistible demands for Life's continuance and renewal. The human being, the most evolved of living animals, must still succumb and surrender to the instinct born at the dawn of evolution.

Besides the human attempt to subdue instinct, the human also tries to exploit instinct to obtain personal pleasure and gratification. But instinct shrugs off the pleasure-seekers; it cares only for its own accomplishment. We who think we will use sex for our own gratification are ourselves only the means to the gratification of Life's loving of itself.

Whether in the self-frustrating attempt to suppress or in the manipulation of instinct to obtain gratification, instinct may become a human neurosis.—(Yes, Freud did find the root of neurosis in sex.)—If we want what we want with an obsessive craving, we will find the act itself wanting. As if

Nature's top priority were pleasing each and every one of us in our self-indulgent sense of need. Absolute personal satisfaction is unattainable, because Nature has no interest in it.

Yet, we persist in attempting control and, especially, exploitation.

177

For the individual human being, coitus is but an episodic intimacy with that sexual essence he or she lacks. Male penetrates femaleness; female absorbs maleness. But neither can incorporate the other, nor can any mutual sexual transubstantiation be effected. What the unconscious most yearns for—permanent commingling and fusion, full completeness—physical sexual acts cannot accomplish. Thus we are sexually insatiable.

Insatiable. With that characteristic Christian spite and envy of pagan genius, St. Jerome libeled the great poet Lucretius by telling the tale that Lucretius committed suicide after an overdose of an aphrodisiac. Sexual need leads to madness and eventual damnation, according to the fanatic celibate Church Father.

Better the insatiable madness of love than the erotic fascination with self-frustration, pagans would retort; better a dose of Lucretius' aphrodisiac potion than the cup of virgin-martyr's blood proffered by Jerome.

Lucretius has been my exemplar for both philosophy and literature. How poignantly he portrays, in the fourth book of *De Rerum Natura*, our all-too-human mania: (I quote from the R. E. Latham translation.)

"Body clings greedily to body; moist lips are pressed on lips, and deep breaths are drawn through clenched teeth.....Their limbs are un-nerved and liquefied by the intensity of rapture..."

As Lucretius writes so beautifully about the intensity of passion, so does he, in a few moving words, about its cyclic futility:

"At length...there comes a slight intermission in the raging fever. But not for long. Soon the same frenzy returns...All to no purpose. One can glean nothing from the other, nor enter in and be wholly absorbed, body in body..."

Our desire for our complement and completion we can satisfy only episodically and spasmod-ically. Coitus, though it relieves tension of the physical drive, never alleviates our awareness of the painful schism between the sexes, the irre-mediable schism.

The coming-together is not a becoming-one.

The sexes do not merely want each other, they want to become each other permanently, while still retaining their own given sex. They want wholeness. That is an impossible, a futile, a tragic ambition. The myth of Hermaphrodite is the parable of that ambition. The sculpted image of Hermaphrodite portrays in that one body our deepest human longing.

Hermaphrodite is a personification in myth and an embodiment in art of both the phylogenetic process of the evolution of life and the ontogenetic development of the human animal, both processes being a progression from singularity through differentiation. Hermaphrodite recalls, and calls us back to, primordial oneness.

178

What is the longing for Hermaphrodite? And—lingering disquiet and scruple—is it perverse?

By a crude interpretation, Hermaphrodite may be taken as merely a perverse fantasy in which exquisite auto-eroticism is effected by building all sexual structures into a single body.

No, the image of Hermaphrodite is not a mere perverse auto-erotic fantasy. The appeal of Hermaphrodite touches the entire developmental sexuality of the viewer. We are drawn to Hermaphrodite in reminiscence of our progression through the developmental phases of auto-homo-heterosexual longing. We see in Hermaphrodite ourself, our lack, and our longed-for fulfillment. Hermaphrodite dwells in a realm beyond that of Narcissus and Eros.

This is the idolater's hymn:
"Oh, Hermaphrodite,
I am for you, and I long for you.
For what I am
For what I lack,
I love myself in you, and
I love the you in myself!"

In the Sleeping Hermaphrodite, art and the unconscious confront directly, and minister to, our gnawing sense of incompleteness, the dualistic separation of the sexes, our human halfness. Our deepest human craving is the physical and psychological craving for total communion between man and woman. Ancient pagan imagination made a spectacular leap of insight when it created Hermaphrodite to heal the fracture, to reunite. Hermaphrodite, the man-woman, the complete human being.

What the modern mind finds so disconcerting about Hermaphrodite is its carnal explicitness. The classical was carnal, and it is difficult for us to get over our Christian moral aversion to pagan explicit honesty. But Hermaphrodite is not physical, not a matter of genitals, hormonal quirks, or congenital peculiarity. Hermaphrodite is not a bisexual specimen, but an androgynous symbol, not a miscarriage but a masterpiece, not Nature's error, but an achievement in human self-understanding. Hermaphrodite is steeped in psychological significance. It touches something basic in our human nature.

Hermaphrodite is a key to the mystery of instinct, the prime dynamic of Life. The fusion of opposites is the ultimate mystery. Hermaphrodite may be one of the deepest psychological truths ever discovered.

180

Having recognized, and ministered to, the affliction of human halfness, the ancients then rejected their solution to the problem. They recoiled from synthesis. Something in the beauty of Hermaphrodite, something in the idea, so repelled the Greeks that they concluded their myth with the dire warning that any man who bathed in the spring where Hermaphrodite dwelt would be stricken with total impotence. Hermaphrodite was relegated to a minor character in the mythology, the idol reduced to use as a garden fertility symbol.

That was a paradox of longing and a rejected fulfillment of longing. Sexual synthesis did not supplant the polarity of Apollo and Aphrodite in the psychology of the pagan mind.

It was instinct itself that recoiled. Did the pagans intuit that the hoped-for fulfillment was actually a retrogression, if not back to the primordial cell, at least to a dead end? Was the sleep of the Sleeping Hermaphrodite actually a death?

Despite the powerful human wish for incorporation into the opposite sex, for fusion, for corporal and psychological transubstantiation, the pagans' restless dynamism compelled them to reject the utter extinction of instinct that is represented by Hermaphrodite. They persisted in the provocative, tense polarity of Apollo and Aphrodite. After all, if Hermaphrodite were real, what then? If you crave the impossible all, you may lose the halfness that you are. And how can we be other than what we are?

181

And so, Hermaphrodite has become an orphan-child of the imagination, a waif that I happened upon in a Roman museum. Our deepest human longing can never be satisfied. Complete and permanent union between the sexes is an impossible aspiration, a mere alluring fantasy. Hermaphrodite attracts, but only as a passing infatuation whose inadequacy we soon perceive, as did the ancients. Hermaphrodite does not seduce us, either.

We look upon the Sleeping Hermaphrodite and upon the poignance of our human nature. But we must stand back, we must keep away, neither to touch nor to embrace nor to love.

Historically, the Sleeping Hermaphrodite is an indication of the turmoil of the Hellenistic Age, the context of the culture of ancient imperial Rome. As the parochial belonging of the *polis* gave way to the values miscegenation of Cosmopolis, the mind went into shock. Oriental mystery religions ran roughshod over the old clique of divinities on Olympus.

What a period of ferment that was, the age that brought about the birth of the cosmopolitan mind. There were titanic cultural struggles between superstition and rationality, myth and science, between idealism and skepticism, between fantasies and reality. Like our own, it was an introspective age, a time of obsessive search for solutions to the problems of the human soul.

It was Christianity that was to provide the enduring answer to the problem unsuccessfully dealt with by the myth of Hermaphrodite, that is, the problem of sex and instinct.

The Christian solution was repression. Christianity launched a campaign to extinguish sexual polarity (no longer male and female, but *brothers and sisters*) and to replace provocative attraction by the cult of virginity, an utterly desexualized celibacy of both body and mind. Let your yearning be to unite your soul with God, not to unite the male body with the female body, Christianity preached with fervid zeal; sublimate *eros* (sexual desire) into *agape* (brotherly love). Christianity declared ideological warfare upon instinct itself.

Just a few Hermaphrodite idols eluded the iconoclastic hammers of the triumphant Christians to tantalize us still. Hermaphrodite remains a vivid symbol of our human longing for wholeness. At the same time, the Sleeping Hermaphrodite depicts the weariness of the Hellenistic Age, a desire for respite, for sleep, for oblivion. And isn't that what our age too wants,—wholeness, but also respite, sleep, oblivion?

182

After having devoted my days to idolatry in the sculpture galleries of Rome, I have unriddled the mystery of *the Incarnation:*—

After the mind, through biological evolution, superseded the body, it then reverted to the body in aesthetic longing. The most humanistic culture is somatic, *somatophilic,* as strikes us immediately when we stand before classical Greek sculpture.

Incarnation means to give bodily form to, to embody. Whereas in Christian theology *the Word became flesh* (idea-into-body), in classical paganism the idea of the divine became the ideal body in the sculpted forms of the god Apollo and the goddess Aphrodite. Classical sculpture is a pagan variation on the Incarnation.

I have found in classical sculpture a profound and sublime embodiment of divine spirit, as well as of human psychology. Pagan sculpture is a theophany. I am in awe, as I behold the image of the naked body, that seemingly frail, mortal, human frame now transfigured into a symbol of immortal divinity. Apollo and Aphrodite are divine beings entered into, incarnated in, beautiful human bodies. The idea was made flesh, hewn in imperishable marble:—The Incarnation.

Iconoclasts and other death lovers are correct in shunning every image as an idol. Aesthetic attraction to corporal sculpture is an idolatry, even an erotic idolatry. The idolater worships and loves the human body, idol of the cult of Life.

The most abundant artifacts here in Rome are pagan statues and Christian relics, the former idols of Life, the latter fetishes of death. Why should we abandon the pagan cult of Life in favor of the Christian cult of death, even if, historically, the demoralized, world-weary culture of ancient societies did so?

Christianity infected sex with guilt, judged Life Itself a sickness to be cured by death. It smashed the idols to bits and inseminated the cultural environment with necrotic relics in its campaign of death-against-Life. The few pagan statues that survived by chance refute the death cult and recall us to amorous worship of Life.

The ancient Greek and Roman pagans were somatophiles, enamored of the wholesome body and its life. If they reduced the divine to the human, didn't they also raise the human to the divine? Their version of the Incarnation was an apotheosis of the human body. Isn't Apollo, gazing out at us from his exquisite human body, a worthy god still? Doesn't the allure of the naked Aphrodite beckon us to lifeloving appreciative vitality?

Christian anticarnalism was an antivitalism. That is why pagan Mediterranean culture, which was so thoroughly somatophilic, vitaphilic, is to be valued and cherished. After two millennia of the purgatorial suffering from Christian morbidity and mortification of the flesh, and living as we do in the inert, mechanical world of our contemporary technosphere, we need to gaze in awe and worship of Apollo and Aphrodite to love our bodies and our lives once again. The body is not the nemesis of spirituality. As the pagans believed, the body is the incarnation of the divine within us.

183

I pause in the pursuit of my theme to wonder what it is that I am up to.

One of the ironies of intellectual history is that the secrets of biological and social dynamics seem to be discovered only after they may be no longer operative. Analytical genius lags; it expresses itself anachronistically.

To give some examples:—

Charles Darwin grasped the mystery of evolutionary adaptation to environment in the nineteenth century, when, because of the advancing technology of the Industrial Revolution, man was already well along in altering, or even eradicating natural environment, if it did not suit his purposes. The theory of evolution no longer applied to the current reality of Darwin's time, which was characterized more by extermination of species, abrupt willed extinction, and by transformation of natural environment into technosphere, than by any process of gradual, random evolution wholly within Nature. Darwin only discovered an outmoded dynamic.

At the same time, Darwin's contemporary, Karl Marx, expounded the notion of class-struggle as a universal explanation of the prime dynamic of human social history. There again was a Johnny-come-lately. Class struggle? The stratified societies of feudalism or aristocracy were past or passing. The increased productivity and wealth of Europe were creating a social mobility that made the entire concept of class old-fashioned, except in the petty consumeristic sense of *keeping up with the Joneses.* There was no motivation to destroy a class to which an individual aspired.

A further instance of the laggard pace of analysis in relation to reality is our own twentieth-century monomania and obsession with sex. I have taken D.H. Lawrence and Sigmund Freud as the most prominent of the unriddlers. I now wonder whether they were not so much prophets as elegists. Both of them may have just talked a dying dynamic to death.

Intense interest and progress in understanding seem to occur only when the dynamic is so moribund that it can no longer conceal its secrets. Whenever we hear a new, original explanation of some dynamic, then, let us ask whether that dynamic is still vital and operative, or whether the thinker is merely reading a few last words over the corpse. (Might that apply to the new science of ecology?)

Furthermore, whenever emerging genius turns attention to a subject, let us tremble in fear at the imminence of some decadence and disintegration. The analytical genius is a pathologist or autopsist, an expert on morbidity and death; he takes as his task the issuance of the death certificate and the composition of the requiem.

What disquieting thoughts, these, as I turn my own analytic attention toward instinct. Is this, my own writing, yet another example of autopsy of a dead dynamic, just another requiem?

184

What do you think about instinct? I mean, what is your valuation of it, specifically, your moral valuation?

You might answer that instinct is a given, like the law of gravity or sunrise-in-the-east, sunset-in-the-west. Why exercise valuation upon a given? Instinct is the dynamic of Life, part of the context within which we live. So we must accept, but there is no point in judging.

That answer won't do, sorry. We are not primitives or pagans anymore. There are no more Dionysia or bacchanalia or rustic revelries, even here in Italy, where once they were the spirit of a people. No, we are Christian, and scientific to boot. Either as Christians or as rationalists, we must put a moral and critical analytical valuation upon instinct.

According to Christianity, instinct is the devil's dynamic, the cause of the Original Sin that has contaminated the soul of every human being that has come onto the earth since Adam and Eve. (If the Original Sin was disobedience, why did Adam and Eve suddenly become ashamed of their nakedness and put on the fig leaves?)

To the Christian, instinct is a source of sin. What is *lust* but instinct? We should be ashamed of our nakedness and of our naked appetites. They seduce us away from spirituality, they corrupt the *immortal soul.* Man is *concupiscent,* that is, susceptible to temptation, which leads to sin, then to eternal damnation; and it is animal instinct that is to blame.

We were made in *the image of God*, the Christians insist, not as just another species of animals. It is our duty to God, as well as in our own self-interest (*salvation*) that we subject instinct to lifelong control. Our spiritual task is to repress, suppress, the animal within us, in order to cultivate detachment and otherworldliness.

As for science, it claims no competence for salvation, but it has retained the religious bias against animal instinct. In the world-view of science, the human being is *the rational animal*, not the instinctual animal. Reason, then, not instinct must be the sovereign. Man is at the apex of the hierarchy of the creatures of the earth—(the same self-estimate, notice, as that in the book of Genesis). Qualitatively different from the animals, we are obligated to act up to our self-estimate. Instinct, infrarational, is suspect, a lower function, not the devil's dynamic to be sure, but bestial nonetheless.

The science of psychology studies instinct, in order to subdue it. If not Original Sin, instinct is an atavistic remnant of animal evolution. The human should be above and beyond it.

As the Christians subjected instinct to *conscience*, so psychologists urge subjecting it to rational control. The *superego* (reason acting as conscience) must conquer the *id* (passions), according to the prescription of Dr. Freud.

So, there for consideration are the moral valuations of religion and science, of the former that instinct is evil, of the latter that instinct is bestial. Heavy negative judgments upon a given.

Why such righteous and severe valuations? Because instinct is within us, it must be recognized, it must be reckoned with, dealt with. Animal instinct intrudes upon our lofty human self-estimate, contradicts it, rebuts our pretensions. Instinct is the ineradicable dynamic of Life Itself, but it is also a subverter of all our metaphysics and our rationalism; it mocks the moral and the mental. The mind, therefore, must retaliate.

Now, certainly, there have been poets, artists, naturalists, and players of the pan flute, to whom instinct, far from being a demon, is a loveable and seductive deity inspiriting Nature and their own nature. Hedonists and irrational ecstatics, they. There is in the National Roman Museum a pagan altar decorated with reliefs of a revelry, an orgiastic homage to instinct. Such abandon embarrasses us moderns. We are moral, we are rational, we are in control.

Now, then, what is your moral valuation of instinct?

185

Let's reconstruct how we came to be as we are and where instinct fits into the scheme of things. Looking back to the origins of Life on earth and to the course that Life has followed, we recount the story as a three-act drama:

ACT I: The primeval earth was inert, a lifeless mass of hot rock rotating and revolving in the clockworks of the solar system. In the beginning was a whirling orb of matter. And upon it precipitated the Great Sea.

ACT II: A spontaneous burgeoning of life spread from the sea to land to air to cover the orb with prolific vitality. A *biosphere* enveloped the *lithosphere*, to use Teilhard de Chardin's mystical neologisms. Life had come upon the earth, generating and regenerating. The dynamic of that process was instinct.

ACT III: The male, now in a necessary role in the generation of life, detached himself from the vital stream of instinct. He created a mind for himself, a mechanistic function separated from instinct and from the female. The male used that mind to gradually construct a counter-Nature. The male has since endeavored to cover over the layer of life with a *technosphere*, a new environmental layer of the human crafted inert.

There you have it, the *Drama of Life on Earth* in three acts, cosmogony, biology, history, and sociology all included.

As we are more interested in destiny than in origins, let us add a postscript to the story, namely, a prophecy:

The world-historical process in essence has been a titanic struggle between male-mind-death on the one hand and female-instinct-Life on the other. Yes, I have introduced a new term, *death.*

The female was, has been, and is the life-force, but the male became a death-force. (I am not making a moral judgment; I am just recognizing the consequence of the defect in the male.)

The mind is the organ of death, and it is the male's organ. That the male mind set itself against female-instinct-Life was a momentous occurrence in evolution.

The human mind is the protagonist of the *Drama of Life on Earth.* That drama is a tragedy and an inevitability. We are now in the final scenes of the third act, proceeding to the terminal and catastrophic postscript.

Life began with a spontaneous impulse. It may perish from a calculated thought.

186

Wait a minute, you might object, isn't the mind as much a part of Nature, a part of human nature, as is instinct?

Learning is natural, certainly. All the creatures of the earth learn; they learn what is essential to their living and their maintenance. Learning facilitates living, enables it, in fact.

The animals study one subject, what we might call empirical natural science, which is merely survival information. A rabbit learns about clover and foxes; the rabbit's curiosity extends not much further than those two alternatives, eating and being eaten. If it is not nourishing, sustaining, or threatening, the animal is seldom much interested, except in a random, playful caprice. Animal learning is utilitarian. No creature except man frenzies about in an unquenchable compulsion *to know*.

Among the animals, learning is the means to living. It must have a specific life-serving application. We may surmise that the primitive human animal, too, began as a self-interested utilitarian learner. However, things and thinking rapidly got out of hand. The human aberration from simple animal learning is what constitutes our evolutionary difference.

Man not only learned about the denizens at the alternatives of eating and being-eaten, like the ungulates and the predators, as they actually were; he also conceived made-up ideas about them. He totemized his fellow-animals and deified the forces of Nature, thus creating religion, metaphysics, the first knowledge completely detached from living.

Each newborn animal must learn about its environment for itself, often with some guidance from its parents, to be sure, but the human transmits acquired learning along with a traditional metaphysics to offspring, and, worse, down to distant generations. The human child is told about life, warned about it, indoctrinated about it, infected with preconceptions that distort later direct experience of it. The human animal learns not only what it experiences directly, but what it has been taught, almost from the day it springs in animal innocence from the womb. Human parents teach useful information, sparing their children some pains, but they also inculcate values, a world-view in fact. Thus, human learning has become mostly detached from direct natural experience. It is encapsulated ideation.

It is not too much to say that no human being ever discovers the world-as-it-is, but, rather, learns much of it in the concepts told by the elders. The survival value of cautionary teaching about wolves and other predators is evident—(but, even there we learn lying propaganda, on the wolf particularly)—; however, the human child has to swallow an entire ideology of pre-digested world-view with the dose of warning. Not only the wolf, but *Almighty God* too.

That we have never been the same since is my basic point. The animals' learning competence is only in the elements of natural environment. The human has plunged ahead and outward into the ever-expanding abstract domains of religion and philosophy, language and law, politics and psychology, aesthetics, science and science-enabled technology, and all the other multitude of created thought systems that occupy the mind of modern man, the enculturated animal. The human attitude toward learning is not the simple animal one of learning in order to live, but—the ultimate transvaluation—living in order to learn. Learning, —that's what life should be!

So, the mind emerged out of Nature, true; but it has fully emancipated itself. The mind stands outside Nature, independent, judgmental, even adversarial. As it has transcended Nature, so now its ambition is to comprehend the whole universe.

Examining the record of its progress so far, how can we doubt its ultimate success?

In the human animal, learning became ideology. And intelligence became intellect.

187

Let us now consider the ascent of mind, of intellect, in the course of evolution and in the chronology of culture.

In the beginning, man was only another animal, with the same instincts as all animals, namely, surviving and thriving. Mind was just a bud.

Early in his evolution, man solved the basic problem of survival. He did so by cunning and by communal organization.

The survival struggle had always been the tonic and stimulus to animal vitality, so man then had to deal with the slack and chronic boredom caused by reduction of the survival struggle, as well as with the phallic energy of male aggression, now excessive to the tasks it faced.

Man undertook a new task, the remodeling of himself. He turned his restlessness and energy inward. He re-created himself as a thinker, cultivating his intelligence until it became intellect.

The intellect is a male instrument, and, because the male's characteristic trait is aggressiveness, man turned the instrument into a weapon. He used his mind to conduct campaigns against various perceived adversaries in the world in which he lived. Knowledge is power, and the male wanted to exercise power.

The first campaign was against matter. Man took inventory of the materials available to him in the environment, learned their properties, and refashioned them into tools useful not only to survival but to further aggressions. He set his brains and hands to tool making,—implements for hunting, then for agriculture, (and for war), all those fabricated artifacts being dug up by archaeologists. Matter was to be exploited. Mind-over-matter is one of the first themes in human history, one of the first muscle-flexing exercises of the developing intellect.

Much further along in the development, the mind became more and more of a directing dynamic of the human. As the mind's self-estimate swelled, the mind began to differentiate humanness from animality, even to try to snuff out the very awareness of our animal nature. Human self-estimate became dephysiologized.

The mind was even to launch a campaign against the body, now considered not as living animal, but as just the form of matter within which the mind, the real human, dwells. You might recall the soul-in-the-cage motif in Greek philosophy or the outright moral repudiation of the body by Calvinistic Christianity.

The paleopsychologists may not be able to tell us exactly when the anticorporal bias of the much later philosophical and religious notions began, but that the tenant yearned to become the landlord we recognize. The body was just another form of matter; it had to be mastered.

Among the animals, intelligence and learning served the body and enabled living. In the human, the body was made to serve the mind, and living enabled learning (the Socratic ideal). The real living was now to be inside a man's head. *The rational animal!*

The human body became a target of attack, because it represented the superseded common animal past. And because the male's relatedness to the female was, as the mind would judge it, the animal one of sex, the body and person of the female were also targeted by the mind. Her body too was out of the animal past that the male mind repudiated and had ambition to transcend. Man achieved the subjugation of woman more by phallic mind than by physical force.

Woman was no pushover as adversary, however. She had as advantage the male's sexual need for her, as well as her indispensability as child producer and nurturer. Besides, women's intelligent perception, *intuition,* was a formidable foe of male analytic intellect.

The male mind has long borne hostility toward the female, the first sex, the primary sex, due to the reality of the male's ultimate dependence upon her. The cultural attack upon woman has been patriarchalism, the ideology of male dominance of the female, a dominance justified by the fantasy of her inferiority.

Besides its campaigns against the visible targets of matter, the human body, and the female, the intellect attacked other forces perceived as adversarial, impalpable forces, namely, the emotions and instinct.

Intellect and emotion work to cross-purposes. A consequence of knowing is not feeling. The more refined the articulation of experience, the less the capacity for direct experience. Mind put itself outside of feeling, resisted submission to emotion, which was now beneath its dignity. The mind scoffed at emotion and feeling; they were the weakness of children and females.

The intellect judged emotions, criticized them, derided them, and, so, hobbled them. Even nurturance and compassion (the finest expressions of natural instinct) were denigrated as just so much more evidence of female weakness. Feeling was objectified. Man became his own psychologist, in order to force feeling to submit.

Ultimately, mind could achieve primacy only if it overcame its most formidable adversary, namely, instinct. Mind could expand only if instinct contracted; it was one energetic against the other in the divided house of the human body. Instinct was of the essence of the animal in the human. Overtly and covertly, the mind worked to check instinct, to suppress it, to eradicate it if possible.

Instinct had long been the energetic of the body, of the animal life and liveliness of the human, as of all other animals. Mind tried to suck vitality out of the body and bottle it up in the brain, it tried to deanimalize, denature the human.

As the intellect hypertrophied, so instinct atrophied. That process has been the essence of the evolutionary history of the human.

In fully developed culture, the ideologies of the intellect—philosophy, religion, psychology—have inculcated the idea that human low-life (*the unexamined life not worth living, sin, neurosis*) was characterized by the corruption of the controlling intellect by the appetites; instinct was perverting.

In fact, it was the other way round. Intellect perverted instinct. That is what our decadence really is.

188

Matter proved mostly nonresistant, the body could be beaten down, the female subjugated, emotion choked, instinct rendered moribund. After those campaigns, the intellect undertook an even more ambitious campaign, total war, in fact. The adversaries now were Nature and Life Itself.

Primitive man suffered from an anxiety of helplessness in the threatening natural environment in which he lived. His mind, his tools, and communal defense enabled him to proceed from vulnerability to adaptation to accommodation, then on to exploitation and control of environment. Man would put Nature in her place.

The goal of that war for mastery over the natural environment has become fully apparent at our end of the chronological spectrum. We have already run fences around, or bulldozed over, the last patches of natural wilderness. Soon we will cover it all over with pavement, the Appian Way in ancient times, the trans-Amazon highway recently; whatever the time period or location, the process is the same, and it is inexorable.

The ultimate goal of the intellect's drive for power is the complete eradication of the natural environment and its replacement by a totally artificial one, an environment that is a complex construct created wholly by human intellect and will: A *technosphere.* The entire earth will be remade by the human.

When the biosphere is gone, Nature herself will be as extinct as many of her creatures have already become. The Latin motto of our technology is *Natura delenda est,* Nature must be destroyed. Never mind the ecological eccentrics, they are indulging themselves in Romantic nostalgia. They will be impotent in their quixotic attempt to obstruct the tide of the war of intellect against Nature.

The intellect is that faculty that exists detached from, and so adversarial toward, Life Itself. The overweening ambition of the intellect to mastery, its boundless drive for power, is directed even against Life Itself. What is Life, but just one more *thing* to be mastered? Science, the tool of the intellect, is the means to the mastery of Life.

The animals, vitalized by lifeloving instinct, commit no exterminations. The animals live wholly within the natural. But the intellect, life-apart, life-deprived, is also anti-Life. It submits even Life to judgment. Its verdict may be "Death!"

The intellect is a self-created autonomous mechanism operating under its own rules, setting its own standard, making decisions according to its own needs. Intellect is monstrous but irresistible. The Gulliver-growth of the intellect, intellectualization, has been the most characteristic fact of our human evolution; we are now fully cerebralized.

The intellect has achieved primacy. And it is totalitarian in its operation.

189

Intellect is in relentless war against instinct. Between the two there will never be reconciliation or higher synthesis. It is necessary, then, to choose one or the other as the personal dynamic of one's life.

Earlier, I challenged you to a valuation of instinct, against the background of the judgments of religion and science. I now challenge to a valuation of intellect, after consideration of some historical background.

What is the standard that we currently set for the worth of a human being? If the worst epithet we hurl at another is *Stupid!*, it would seem that highly developed intellect is the highest-valued quality. We live in an age of the primacy of intellect, in which people are graded from lower to higher according to a cerebral standard, a mathematically stated I.Q. Smarter is superior.

Against such high estimation of intellectualism, we must recognize that most historical societies have valued other traits—family membership and lineage, class, leadership ability, social or managerial skills, and so on—higher, because more conducive to the welfare of society. Hypertrophied minds—the mandarins and monastics—were treated as eccentrics, rather than models to be emulated. (Of course, what I'm arguing against here is not intelligence, but intellectualism. I wouldn't argue against intelligence; I'm too smart for that.)

The hierarchy of our current values goes back to the ancient Greek, or, more correctly, the Socratic bias that the higher life is rationalistic examination and analysis, that rationality is the highest human trait. In the Socratic view, more mind meant a higher quality of living and the brainiest were superior to all others. The intellect was man's only transcendent achievement.

Out of that bias—(actually a self-serving vocational bias of the philosopher)—has come our human self-estimate as *the rational animal.* Indeed, the problem of rationality-versus-irrationality (for which latter word we may read *instinct*) has become tantamount to the war-between-good-and-evil. The philosophical valuation thus approaches the religious one.

Socratic rationalism was a veritable cerebromegalomania. If we consider rationality and irrationality in terms of good-and-evil, however, we find no such simple correlations as the Greek philosophers would have us believe. Ruminate awhile on the evil perpetrated in the name of ideological rationality and you might leap to a revaluation of values.

For, what is an occasional murder, a *crime of passion*, compared to the millions massacred because of such abstract mind-fabrications as *truth, dogma, belief, doctrine, patriot-* and other *isms, honor, just cause, Crusade, Jihad* etc. in warfare organized on the most rationally sophisticated and efficient lines? What was more rationally considered and rationally carried out than the atomic bomb dropped on Hiroshima?

Our historical experience of intolerance, persecution, and massacre of heretics must make us question the philosopher's notion of the hypertrophied mind as the *summum bonum* and the rationalist as the superior human being. The assertion of the primacy of the intellect begins to sound like mere arrogance of an upstart self-created automaton. Considered from the standpoint of morality, the intellect shrinks from no enormity; it relishes its power to even effect nuclear holocaust and world destruction.

Socratic bias reached its most exquisite expression in the pithy Latin motto of Descartes, *Cogito, ergo sum* (I think, therefore I exist.) That is nothing less than the motto, the manifesto, of modern Western man, his very *raison d'être,* to get French for a phrase, in deference to Descartes. Isn't such a notion living gone to the head with a vengeance? A thought of mine, the precondition and proof of my very existence! What, was I nobody and nothing before I picked up pen to dash off *Instinct*? Not *sum*, and then *ergo cogito* (cogitation as a true afterthought!), but the other way around. If an animal doubted its existence, we wonder, would it so demoralize the poor creature as to discourage it from the struggle for survival?

Philosophy is on the side of intellect; well, we could have guessed that from the beginning, the vocational bias again.

How have we perceived the role of intellect in our history, how have we characterized it? In the great saga of mind-over-matter, which comprises much of human history, intellect has been cast in the role of hero.

Yes, in our human historical melodrama, the intellect has been the intrepid hero undertaking Herculean labors against intractable matter, *the secrets of Nature, the unknown,* and so on, un-riddling it all, stripping it bare to enable man to ravish, exploit and plunder for his own benefit. We are all familiar with that theme, *the frontiers of knowledge* panegyric.

Mind propagandizes on behalf of itself; it pre-sents itself as heroic, the best and the good. In defense of its exalted status, the mind attacks pretenders, like intuition (illogical mind), super-stition (incompetent mind) and ignorance (lazy mind).

Even hero has not been enough to satisfy the megalomania of mind. Why not god, or *God*? Indeed, "Mind is that than which none greater can be thought". (Excuse the parody, St. Anselm.)

What blessed Anselm did in his original, "God is that than which none greater can be thought," was not prove the existence of God, as he hoped, but, rather, postulate thinking as proof of existence. Combining Descartes and Anselm, we would get: "I think, therefore I exist. I think He exists, therefore He exists."

Anselm couldn't think of any higher thought than the Omniscient Thinking One. So, human intellectualizing was nothing less than an *imitatio Dei*, not only a higher life, as the Greek philosophers had maintained, but the holy life too. An omniscient *God* was the ultimate validation of intellect as the prime human value.

Theology's *God* was a god of intellect. And of will. Intellect and will, those two posited divine attributes, were (what else?) the two typical male traits projected into metaphysics. (*God*, a thinker, like me! A doer, like me!) *God* as the Supreme Male. *In our own image.*

What about Life? According to theo-mythology, Life came to be as a consequence, not of generation from the female, but as a willed male idea. Not the primordial cell; the primordial thought willed into existence by the spoken command, "Let there be...!".

In Genesis, the process of Creation led up to the grand climax, creation of the human. Life was only the means by which Mind created mind—("And God created man..."), only the middle term through which Perfect Omniscience created perfectible intellect. Mind was the cause, Life the means, new mind ("to know Him") the ultimate purpose of Creation. So runs the Judeo-Christian patriarchal myth.

In Nature, mind was an epiphenomenon of Life. In theology, Life is an epiphenomenon of Mind.

God serves as model and sanction for man's prime value, which is hypertrophied intellect. Criticism of intellect is not only obnoxious, it is now positively blasphemous. There has been nothing less than an apotheosis of intellect.

Against such strong endorsement of intellect by both philosophy and religion, would you be so bold, so unreasonable, so atheistic, as to venture on a contrary valuation?

190

In the past few centuries, science has made a lot of trouble for religion. It is an historical irony that science, the most extreme manifestation of male-mindedness, temporarily restored Life as the supreme value, when it repudiated the Creating Mind of the male cosmogony in the book of Genesis.

Darwinian biology came close to a cult of Life. Its philosophical base was a sort of vital materialism, in which Life created itself, or reproduced and improvised itself, in ever more complex and perfectly adapted patterns. The human mind was only a very late epiphenomenon of Life's random prolificness, an adaptive achievement of evolution.

.....

Or, upon reconsideration, the supreme achievement. Teleology crept back in. As in the religious world-view God created the world so that man, His highest creature, could live in it, comprehend it, exploit it, so evolution kept casting the dice of variations until it hit the jackpot,—the human mind.

In Darwinian biology, the divine mind was banished, but in His stead the human mind was deified. The evolutionary mechanism (*natural selection*) was accessible to manipulation by a greater controlling mechanism, namely, the mind of man. Life could now be subjected to direction; the methods were selective breeding, eugenics, and now genetic engineering. Science asserted the human intellect over Life, and worse, the intellect against Life. The human mind can do a better job of managing Life than Nature has done.

The fractious row between religion and science seems foolish. Each in its own way appeals to right-mind as its fundamental justification (religion to authoritarian mind, science to analytic mind). Each is allied to the male against the female and instinct. Despite their condescension and antagonism toward each other, religion and science are complementary. They should recognize their mutuality and stop condemning each other. After all, they are allies in the same war.

Religion no longer effects much of progressive significance in our modern world. Ascendant science now has its way; it is science that reigns supreme as the mind's anointed. Science has determined our present and will determine our future, by means of technology. The proof of technology is its success; it has achieved much more than prayers ever did.

And what is the future that scientific technology will determine for the earth? I think that science-enabled technology is our Western ritual of protracted hari-kari. There is no such thing as a *good idea*. Every idea has been a dagger plunged into Life, every system a siege against Nature. Each scientific discovery, each innovation in technology, is another piece added to the cunning complexity of our doom-machine.

All thoughts culminate in suicide. We have seen what our past has been. Looking into the future, we perceive our fate. Mind will have mastered It All at last, mastered It All by eradicating Nature.

191

When I was a boy, I was fascinated by animals. I pleaded for and acquired a variety of living pets that I observed, lived with, and related to. I wanted to learn about all the living creatures of the earth. I plunged into my enthusiasm whenever I could, whether it was just in the reading of a picture book in my apartment in Chicago or in exploration of Nature in my neighborhood or on trips to parks, farm fields, and woods. I thought of myself as a living animal, one of them. I felt affinity, relatedness, love, and belonging. A naturalist, I was fascinated by Life and by my own participation in it. I lived within the context of Nature.

Today's children, I observe, are fascinated by things. As indoors creatures, their relatedness is to man-created objects, electronic devices. What they fantasize about is not adventures among the animals of the living world, but acquisition and manipulation of devices that they direct against other human beings and their devices or out against the world in general.

Today's children do not live in the present of Nature; they live in a surreal fantasy of a sci-fi future in which Nature has ceased to exist. They see themselves, not in the context of Nature, but in the context of the technosphere. Their sensitivity is technologized. They are technophiles.

There was some destructiveness in my relatedness to Nature, I admit. I killed insects for mounting, I fished, I shot birds. Some of that destructiveness was taught to me in school; they called it science. Fortunately, I never took a biology class in which Nature is learned by dissecting a frog; that experience would have corrupted my sensitivity. I didn't want to be on the outside looking in; I wanted to be a participant, a part of It All.

The fascinations and play and fantasies of today's children seem to me to be totally about destructiveness. Children do not develop a sense of empathy for, and belonging to, the living world.

Instead, detached, they want manipulation and mastery, even unto extermination of all obstructions to their willfulness. They fantasize weapons to kill indiscriminately, every other living being, until they are left with...what? Only themselves and their weapons.

And when the child becomes adolescent and the erotic drive arises, what happens then? Already enamored of the inert, adolescent males merge their sexuality not into animal identity and belonging-to-Nature, but, rather, into technological manipulativeness and the urge-to-kill. Erotic drive is their new weapon for mastery and domination.

The play of our childhood prefigures, maybe even determines, the work of our adulthood. And our childish attitudes and activities persist into our maturity. The way that the child perceives Life and Nature—(so difficult is it to cure ourselves of our upbringing)—continues into adulthood. Will our children, when grown up, feel any respect-of-belonging, or will they consider Life and Nature mere things for their exploitation, dispensable when no longer useful?

Can we observe our children's development without being alarmed at what they are becoming?

192

The modern mind must tinker and tamper with everything; it wants to explain It All. Nothing is just left alone. Every problem must be solved. The ambition of the modern mind is to reduce Life to rational, manipulatable formulae.

Life without any mystery,—that is the life to which modern man aspires. But is his life, is his liveliness, I wonder, in any way improved or enhanced by relentless labors of analysis? Is mastery a better life than mystery?

As the biologist who vivisects an animal thereby kills it, so a man who analyzes and explains a phenomenon destroys that phenomenon, and, incidentally, also destroys his own capacity for appreciation of it. We may love a woman in her every part and particle, but if we seek to solve her we must perforce tear her apart in the process. Left with nothing but the dissected scraps of her offal, we feel, then, not love and fascination but revulsion and disgust. The practice of vivisection contaminates the life of the practitioner.

I am not objecting to curiosity or to practical learning. What I am objecting to is the pathological mania-to-explain, which has become a pre-eminent trait of the modern mind, explanation as an end-in-itself. (I myself do not explain; I speculate or report or warn.)

What primitives understand but we do not is that it is only by the sense of wonder that we can approach an intuitive comprehension of the everyday miracle within which we live. Myth, the outburst of fascination, is human homage to that mystery. Modern man, however, is too sophisticated, too scientific, too rational, to listen to the wisdom of the old mythmakers. He thinks that, compared to himself, they were naïve simple-tons.

And so, our contemporary scientist prattles on mechanically, deluding himself that the clinking and sputtering of his comic cerebral engine is a soaring blast deep into the outer and inner in-finite.

193

What the human being of our age needs is not the fabrication of ever-new ideas, but, rather, a method for the rediscovery of old, long-lost, sensi-tivities.

194

Nietzsche's concept of a will-to-power is the energetic applicable to what I am writing about, a will-to-power in a psychological, as well as in a biological, sense.

The evidence of evolution and observance of the universal struggle for survival validate the biological aspect of a will-to-power. Animals assert themselves against others of their own kind and against other species they encounter. Survival is competitive. Life wants to survive and thrive. So the biological will-to-power. But what about a psy-chological will-to-power?

I once came across an interpretation of the Nietzschean concept perpetrated by the psycho-analyst Alfred Adler, who asserted that the will-to-power is a fundamental male drive. Dr. Adler said that man as male must *get on top of* woman, force her to submit to him, and, in that way, successfully exercise his will-to-power. To be assured of his potency (as long as we are speaking in sexual terms), man must get on top of woman.

(We tropical denizens, who have been seduced and reduced by Amazonian she-cats, do not take such crude male-assertiveness seriously, because we have learned our lessons from life. Nonetheless, let's address ourselves to the notion:)

To derive a sense of power by means of physical dominance over the weaker female body seems to me a flight from powerlessness, a desperate attempt to dispel the anxiety of impotence. The man who feels himself a man only when he looms over, holds down, and exploits a woman is a half-man, a not-yet-man. One cannot achieve manhood by vandalism against womanhood.

The male adolescent notion that sex is something that a man takes from a woman is one of the most pernicious of our perversities. Men whose attitude toward woman is one of conquest remain retarded all their lives. That kind of will-to-power is a mere delinquent bullyism. Woman is not a trophy; predatory success is not true power. Priapism is the lie that impotence tells itself.

All that a man will ever learn about sex is what the women in his life, from his mother on, teach him; by himself, a man will not even have dim inklings. What I have learned, what women have taught me, is that instinct is the power that overpowers all pretensions to power.

If a will-to-power is a prime human behavioral dynamic—and I am inclined toward the idea—, how are we to apply it, then, to the relations between the sexes? Must man overcome woman, in order to feel sexual fulfillment? (Or, in feminist terms, must woman *get on top of* man?) Is the will-to-power really only a will-to-hurt (or, in feminist woman, a will-to-revenge)?

The answer to that question is that the ultimate exercise of the will-to-power is a willed acquiescence to the powerlessness of total surrender to instinct. The most potent are those who are able to yield to thralldom; they are able to will willlessness. A man who has attained an all-pervading sense of power no longer craves power. He can, powerfully, yield up himself to his woman and to the tidal current that sweeps them both away.

Neither sex must attempt to subdue the other, because to subdue is to conquer and crush. Man and woman must not commit predation against each other.

No. The ultimate of the human sense of power is the strength secure enough to let go. We must submit to each other and go with the flow of instinct, that current of life and health within us. Dr. Adler's prescription was actually a description of our pathology.

Like intellect, willfulness too is the enemy of instinct. We must let go. As much as the will-to-power is a will-to-love, it must do as love wills.

Have I learned, Maria Heléna?

195

Man is manic to explain. And he inflicts a brutish will-to-power upon woman, upon all Nature, in fact. Another affliction of the human animal, a human perversion of the will-to-power, is what I call the *compulsion-to-control*. We want to know everything, only in order to control everything. We feel most powerful, we feel fulfilled, when we exercise control.

Animal will-to-power is rooted in instinct; its goal is survival. The compulsion-to-control, however, is cerebral and calculated; the only need it meets is a psychological one. The male, anxious about impotence, asserts his potency through exercising control.

The compulsion-to-control is directed against the old adversaries of intellect, namely, against matter, against the female, against instinct, against the environment and Nature, ultimately against Life. The compulsion-to-control turns matter into tools, the female into chattel, instinct into extinct, environment into workshop, Nature into property, and Life into death. The only thing left untouched by the compulsion-to-control is itself.

The compulsion-to-control is the relentless campaign to exploit, use, abuse, subdue, and, if deemed necessary, eradicate. The entire history of the human is nothing but the record of achievement of the compulsion-to-control, in all its many aspects, from primitive tool making to the destructive incursions of our contemporary technology against Nature.

Rome itself is a Capitol of the compulsion-to-control. The ancient Universal Empire and the continuing Universal Church are two Roman efforts in the campaign of the compulsion-to-control.

Man has valued his life as a doing, rather than as a being and becoming; he craves productivity beyond the animal dropping of offspring. To do is to live. The most gratifying kind of doing is exercising control.

All the artifacts of the past, all the many manufactures of the present, all the inert contrivances of our expanding technosphere are the inventory accumulated by the compulsion-to-control.

Everything that has been done and made by man can be accounted for by that drive to mastery, the compulsion-to-control. And that compulsion—the insight leaps out at us—is nothing other than intellect-driven will waging war against the world. ("God blessed them, saying to them…'Fill the earth and conquer it. Be masters of the fish of the sea, the birds of heaven and all living animals on the earth'…")

After the male has learned in order to control, after he has achieved control, then what? He loses his fascination and destroys, to go on to further learning and further control. (The insect bottled becomes boring; let's kill it and collect another one.) The compulsion, impelled by the male's defectiveness and anxiety about impotence, is inexorable. (Go, therefore, and exterminate as you will. Capture all the animals and slaughter them in the Colosseum.) The ultimate consequence of the compulsion-to-control is the death of all that man touches.

"Live-and-let-live" is an obsolete directive. All must now submit to ravishment by the male mind and will. What resists will be destroyed. What submits will be destroyed, too.

196

No postulated dynamic or energetic can be claimed as a prime source of human motivation if it is merely directed toward the outer world, leaving the inner being untouched.

Nietzsche was aware of that. He considered self-overcoming the highest expression of the will-to-power. Nietzsche held up the monk, the ascetic—(in vulgar estimation the most impotent class of men)—as the perfect type and exemplar of the will-to-power, because the ascetic masters that most indomitable of adversaries, namely, oneself.

It seems ironic that Nietzsche, who so assailed the tyranny of religion over the mind of man, should nonetheless put forward as his *overman* (*homo optimus*) the one who most thoroughly tyrannizes himself. The overman is the ultimate self-created, self-directed, but also self-subdued human being.

So, the will-to-power is directed as much inward as outward. Similarly, my concept of the compulsion-to-control. *Control yourself!* is the first commandment directed toward the child. That instilled compulsion permeates our attitude toward ourselves for the lifetime thereafter.

There are those who, denying *free will*, doubt whether self-control is possible. I doubt, or rather I repudiate, self-control itself. Self-control is a self-subduing, a self-throttling. As I said before, to subdue is to conquer and crush. . .(But then I myself am a wayward type.)

Self-control is one of the most highly valued character traits of modern rational man, who has no tolerance for spontaneity. How pervasive is the compulsion-to-control? Why, it extends itself out to the infinite horizons of the universe and into the core of the human soul. Space exploration is its outer reach. Its inner reach, its most intimate incursion, is perpetrated by psychoanalysis.

197

This is what I first thought psychoanalysis was:—

The psychoanalytical perspective is that the study of human psychology should be directed toward the entrances and exits of the body. The human person is to be understood according to how he or she has reacted to the physiological occurrences, influxes and effluences, at the mouth, eyes, nose, ears, urethra, vagina, and anus. Psychoanalysis naturalized understanding of the human being. If you seek to understand personality and behavior, it said, examine responses to what enters and leaves the body.

Study nourishment, elimination, sexuality,—the oral, the anal, and the genital.

That return to acknowledgement of human animality seemed to me a refreshing rebuttal to the religious and philosophical doctrine of the human occupying, rather than being, the body.

According to psychoanalysis, the adult is to be understood as the product of developmental reactions to the passing-through of animal sensations. Psychological processes stem from physiological processes.

Psychoanalysis seemingly returned man to earth and to the animal kingdom. Goodbye metaphysics, let's get back to biology.

198

Of course it's not that simple. Psychology cannot be reduced to physiology, even the mechanistic, deterministic physiology of psychoanalytic conception. Psychoanalysis wanted to be a depth psychology, so it had to probe deeper. In doing so, it acquired an overweening ambition.

Freud, let us remember, was a Jew; Judaic moralism would have to assert itself somewhere in the system. Paradoxically, Freud was also an exegete of the Greek myths, a mythmaker himself, and an avid collector of pagan classical sculpture—(a renegade Jew in so surrounding himself with pagan idols). Like Aristotle taking on classical tragedy, Freud would explain the myths in rational terms.

First, the mythology of religion. Primitive religion had as its goal the propitiation of powerful divinities and the attempt, through the bribe of rites and sacrifices, to control the divine powers to the benefit of man. (The Latin formula was *Do ut des*, I give to the god so that the god gives to me.) Unfortunately, prayers and sacrifices proved unavailing against misfortune, the gods unamenable or unsusceptible to human direction.

That goal of religion was given up, abandoned as mere *superstition*. The gods could not be controlled. The compulsion-to-control, however, remained powerful in the human mind. So, religion gradually turned from the futile attempt to control the gods to a moderately successful attempt to control the relations between human beings (*commandments*) to the ultimately more successful attempt of the human being to control oneself.

Judaic morality, after due deference to the homage due the Creator, directed itself into prohibitions of harmful social interrelatedness. Christianity then came along to personalize and psychologize religion by imposing a discipline of self-surveillance and self-control through the notions of *sin* and *guilt* and the stern internal enforcer, *conscience.*

What was it within the human being that needed control? Why, it was instinct, renamed *Original Sin,* revealing itself through *concupiscence* (a tendency to sin, sinability). Christianity declared war on instinct. Instinct, it indicted, was evil; it had to be throttled, caged, killed off if possible.

Dr. Freud, a self-conscious secular Jew, dismissed religion as an *illusion* with no future, yet he himself was a moralistic Jew of ancient type. The goal of psychoanalysis, as he proclaimed it as if just descended from Sinai, was *to make the unconscious conscious* (the mania-to-explain, again) and, beyond that, to force the deep dark lower forces (*id*—Latin *it*—, new name for instinct) to submit to the halter of higher faculties, (*ego*, rationality or *superego*, neo-Latin scientific terminology for Judeo-Christian *conscience*).

Psychoanalysis proclaimed its own particular compulsion-to-control. It would succeed where religion had failed. It would subdue instinct at last.

If Christianity had already diabolized sexuality, psychoanalysis added further items to the indictment, then offered itself as the only true, modern, scientific, effective exorcism. (That it would turn its devil into an idol is a subject I will have to consider shortly.)

To make the unconscious conscious:—But psychoanalysis never questioned whether that would be a good thing, conducive to health; it just assumed it. Psychoanalysis claimed, for example, that the dream was therapeutic only if translated into rational terms; but what if dream interpretation is an intrusion that actually frustrates the self-therapy of the unconscious in dreams? Well, never mind, the most important thing is that the human being must be explained. *Analysis* is the second part of the word, *psychoanalysis.*

As for its assault upon instinct, seconding the earlier efforts of Western religion, psychoanalysis never asked itself whether neurosis might actually be in the assault of the compulsion-to-control upon instinct, not in instinct itself. To subdue is to conquer, crush, even unto a kill.

Freud was a prophet of Old Testament type, but he was also a devotee of classical paganism,— paradoxical combination in any individual. (What strange tour wouldn't Freud as *ciceróne* conduct of the sculpture galleries of Rome!) Rationalist through and through, Freud would explain the myths.

Why, they are not myths at all; they are clinical descriptions of *complexes*, an Oedipus in us all. But where the Greek myths were all about promiscuous interrelatedness among gods, goddesses, humans, and the creatures of the animal kingdom in the context of cosmic Nature, Freud's new mythology was about conflicts between psychological constructs,—*id, ego, superego, libido, pleasure principal, reality principal, death-instinct,* etc.—within the mind of the human being. A personalized psychological mythology. Titanic battles going on inside of us, heroic struggles, with tragic outcomes, however, because Freud was a pessimist, like the Greek tragedians.

Instead of faraway ancient Olympus or Thebes, the present, proximate human mind. In his mythology, Freud replaced the primordial past of the cosmos with the personal past of biographical childhood. Of course the past determines the present. Creation myths are stories to explain how the world came to be as we now find it. Freud's tales of infantile perversion explain how the human person came to be as he or she is. For Freud the pessimist, the past was to blame. Damn, *Original Sin*, all over again!

Psychoanalysis offered itself as the means to mental health. As if relentless analysis, stirring up inner conflict, setting the human being against oneself, poisoning self-estimate, raising the compulsion-to-control to a prescriptive mandate, and wallowing in a deterministic pathological past constituted the means to health.

199

We moderns are as fascinated with the psychoalytic mythology as the ancients were with their own. Too bad our mythology has more demons than divinities.

Freud once told a folksy anecdote about a horse that was the pride of a small Bavarian village. It was a magnificent animal, could perform tremendous feats of strength, but unfortunately it ate too much. Although the villagers loved their horse, they resented its costly upkeep. So they decided to reduce its ration by a few stalks of hay each morning. They thus tapered down the ration of the horse, who, with its horsey simple-mindedness, could not figure out what was being done to it. Finally, the villagers had the animal down to a ration of nothing. The horse suddenly died, and the villagers hadn't the slightest notion why.

That may be what we are doing to our instinct,—starving it out.

Let me offer another possibility in this parable:—

A family in Africa had acquired an orphaned lion cub and undertook to domesticate the snarling little beast. Things went well until the house walls got to be too confining for the now-grown lion. It disturbed the neighbors with its roaring and took to cuffing the children around a little too roughly. Despite that, the family owned the lion as their pet and would not turn it loose. They decided to taper off its ration every day, hoping that as it became weaker it would be more docile and better house-mannered. On the day when the ration had been reduced to a saucer of watered milk, the lion gave out a mighty roar and attacked and ate every last member of the family. With its new strength, the lion escaped from the house and terrorized the whole village.

If we attempt to subdue instinct, we might starve it to death.

Or we might provoke it to desperate and destructive raging.

200

The rampant sexual pathology of our contemporary society has not gone unnoticed, either by moralizers or diagnosticians. Our derangement is

[72]

too blatant to be denied or ignored. The daily news is all child abuse, molestations, sexual harassment and assault, and even sex-involved murder.

Whether the moralists' religious strictures are the answer to it all I doubt. As for the elaborated diagnoses, they themselves partake of the very symptoms of the malady. Psychoanalysis has now systematized an entire catalog of neuroses of instinct, mostly sexual. (By *neurosis*, psychoanalysis means the case of nerves that we are all suffering from.) It then proposes to cure neuroses with the very factor that was the pathogen, namely, intellect-directed willfulness, manipulative male cerebralism. The therapy is, in fact, a reinfection.

Psychoanalysis tells modern man what is wrong with him, analyzes and rationalifies sexuality, thereby intensifying the sickness. But how articulate the sick one becomes about his pathology, how much self-understanding (and self-indulgence)! The terminally ill patient discourses learnedly (though helplessly) about the etiology of his affliction. To know about sickens, and that kind of knowing about but sickens all the more.

What we actually suffer from—(and this is the theme of my chapter)—is not instinct, but intellect, the mania-to-explain, and willfulness, a runaway will-to-power, the compulsion-to-control, mandated self-suppression, in short, our science, our technology, our therapeutics.

Freud the liberator was, in reality, Freud the corruptor. The opposition that some women show to the ideology of psychoanalysis, to the *penis envy* doctrine and the rest, is a sound self-defensive instinct. Women may still have some remnant of healthy instinct, even if men have lost it utterly. Freud was a formidable champion of the male; he was one-of-the-boys, swaggering with his cigar. He delivered a devastating blow against the female, as he did against instinct.

Freud was not a proponent of sex, as he has been misrepresented; he was an enemy of instinct. He launched a relentless campaign against the natural, his ideology and therapeutic methodology both insidious and corrupting. Like all heroes of the intellect, Freud committed villainy against Nature.

201

Well, I'm worn out by the turbulence I've subjected myself to in plunging into the maelstrom of instinct. My head hurts, but I carry on to a conclusion by considering one more topic I had promised to treat:—

Psychoanalysis, like Milton with his Lucifer, turned its devil into an idol. Despite the righteous moralism of its founder, psychoanalysis made proclamation that *libido* rules, with the logical inference that human beings must submit to the ruler.

But psychoanalytic *libido* is not instinct; it is a sexualized will-to-power.

The psychoanalytic determinism of drive justified every perversion. The list that it put together as a catalog of neuroses we now take as a description of varieties of normal human behavior. (Give it name, and it becomes familiar.) We are coming to accept the pathological, the cruel, even the criminal, as normal and inevitable; (in fact, they are our favorite entertainment). We are inured to our own affliction and increasingly tolerant of, and indulgent of, the afflictions of others. Never before has self-destructive, mutually destructive behavior had such a sophisticated scientific rationale. "That's what we really are."

It is ironical that Freud succeeded in freeing us from the bonds of *repression*, only to perpetrate a re-enslavement to a more corrupting bondage, namely, obsession with, and indulgence of, diseased drive. Repressed no more, we will unleash ourselves. What Freud has loosed turns out to be a raging lion among us.

Psychoanalysis, a reputed therapy, has itself become a pathogen in the individual and a carcinogen in society. It wrote *man* in lower case, *Sex* in upper case, promoting the subservience of the former to the latter. And, in the manner of a self-fulfilling prophecy, it has become so.

Psychoanalysis is a vehicle of decadence. Not because it dared to treat a subject considered taboo by prudish Victorians, but because it idolized *libido*—(not healthy instinct, but diseased drive)—and debased the human being in the process. In psychoanalysis, we have gotten a pornographic psychology at last. Psychoanalysis has provided the rationale for our brutalization. And we are becoming what it told us we are.

Aberrations

[Readers: Here is much of what is wrong with instinct in the human.]

202

The problem of human sex, or, should I say, the human problem of sex is due to the biological fact that our sexual drive emerges too early, demands unrelentingly, and is overwhelming.

The girl at eleven years old, the boy at thirteen,—both are still children. Their emotions are childish, their brains undeveloped, their behavior impulsive. Then, with so many of their own developmental challenges still ahead, they suddenly undergo a sexual awakening. Those now sexualized children struggle to cope with disturbing hormones and urges they cannot comprehend or control.

Attempting to help (but also restrain) them, we offer a sex education in which the lesson in anatomy and physiology is immediately followed up with a dire warning about venereal diseases. Throw a fright into the youngsters; maybe that will dissuade them from too-early sexual experimentation. The statistics on teen pregnancy indicate the failure of that effort to make the biological imperative repulsive. Instinct, once activated, is heedless.

The idea of children as responsible parents is absurd. In despite, sexual urges impel them toward procreation. The sexual precocity of the human sets in motion the lifetime of human sexual problems.

Many other animals have a periodicity to their sexual activity, as in rut and estrus. Such timing is usually attuned to the seasons when procreation and rearing of young have the best chance for success. Outside the mating and rearing season, those animals may live the rest of the year free of sexual demands.

Not so the human. Although "In spring a young man's fancy likely turns to thoughts of love", in actuality human sexual readiness and activity are year-round. The human female does have a periodicity of monthly fertility, true, but her receptivity is not restricted to a season; good thing, because the human male is always in rut.

From the first freshet of hormones in adolescence through decades of maturity the human sexual urge is unrelenting. Every day of our lives is full of obsession and fantasies and craving and a quest for opportunity. Even the night provides no respite, because dreams may be erotic. Only old age decrepitude and approaching death provide belated relief.

The human is one of the most highly sexualized of the animals, both in strength and biographical duration of drive. Should we be surprised, then, that overwhelming instinct impels toward excess?

Our moral codes command "Thou shalt not!" for this or that type of sexual behavior. Social mores lay their censure upon disruptions to society resulting from irresponsible liaisons. Nonetheless, we put the thought of Hell out of mind, we cause scandal, because we do what we must do, irrespective of any religious or social attempts to impose control.

Too soon, too constant, too long-lasting, and just too much, the human sexual instinct runs roughshod over us.

203

Philologically speaking, the noun *sex* has no meaning, because there is no such thing, no it-of-sex.

The only accurate description of the phenomenon would be a gerund, a noun-verb, like *sexing*, which would correctly characterize the dynamic, ever-flowing process of instinct.

We fall on our semantic faces when we assert that *sex* is some thing that we have or do. (We even confuse the having and the doing with the idiom *to have sex.*) And there is certainly no *Sex*, capitalized and reified.

It is a linguistic fallacy to talk about *sex*, because there is no such entity. Instead, we should think in terms of *process*, "sexing sexing within us and between us",—phraseology not very elegant, but accurate.

204

It is not surprising that children being raised to value modesty are scandalized when they discover that they were born totally naked. The idea is too foreign to their conception of themselves. They vaguely hold themselves accountable for a sin, or at least an embarrassment to their parents.

Putting small children promiscuously together in a bath is the best and most natural form of sex education they could ever get. The human camaraderie of naked splashing will dispel the obsessive curiosity that makes of the other sex a concealed shame.

If a child has brothers and sisters and loving parents, a happy family and a warm, nurturing home, that child will grow up sexually normal. If those family and home conditions are lacking, there will be deviance, all subsequent efforts at sex education notwithstanding.

There is a single basic cause for the rampant epidemic of incapacity of healthy relatedness in our society, namely, the breakdown of the family. For the consequent emotional orphanism there is no cure. The damage is lifelong and usually incapacitating.

205

Parents used to become appalled when small boys fondled themselves. "Mustn't do that!", they would scold.

Then, to help the boy resist temptation, the parents would give him a gun to play with. Pistol instead of penis,—more wholesome.

The innocent child plays with life. His corrupt parents teach him that death is more fun.

206

Urination and defecation are the losses that are gains for the body,—the idea of the good as disposing of an excess, of finding relief through bodily discharge.

Sexual intercourse as analogous,—feeling better by getting rid of something, by getting something out of the system, by disposing of an inner irritant.

Haven't I heard men talk in such terms,—the female as toilet?

How, then, shall we think of women's sexual desire for men?

207

There is in the Borghese Gallery a statue of Venus of the type of the Capitoline Venus. Examining it this morning with close attention to detail, I discovered that some modern prankster had tampered with the ancient idol by adding a few subtle touches, thus far detected neither by the museum staff nor the tourists.

Between the bare body of Venus and one of her fingers near the pubic area someone had deftly inserted a tuft of black hair. That same or another perpetrator had also penciled on a vertical line in the appropriate place to indicate the pubic cleft. (That particular tampering, incidentally, may be noted on other of the female nudes in the museums, some realist critics correcting the sculptor's idealist anatomical inaccuracy.)

So, Venus has been violated.

What attitude should an aesthete and appreciator take toward such defilement of pure art? A tolerant one, I think. If art is sex gone to the head, we should not be offended that there is occasional relapse back to the basics, a descent to the organic source.

The vandal took a natural reductionist attitude toward the sublimation of the erotic instinct into art. "This is what it's really all about," he said. "Venus is woman, and woman is this:—," adding some anatomical specifics.

All right, he has a point. Of course the goddess is only a woman, after all. A little dose of raw realism may compromise, but it does not abnegate idealism.

The real doesn't offend my aesthetic sense. Venus is as alluring and loveable to me with the explicit female features added. And now her cold stone feels a bit more like warm human flesh.

208

Some men show contempt for women by referring to them in a vulgar terminology that personifies the female genitals or buttocks or breasts and makes those body parts signify the whole person: A woman is only her genitals, all genitals are base and substitutable for sexual purposes, therefore all women are base and substitutable:— That is the logic of the degradation of woman. It is a vicious synecdoche.

If a woman is as base as her most animal sexual parts, so is she as unclean as her most animal sexual function, namely, menstruation. Adolescent boys make crude and contemptuous references to the menstrual process, feigning disgust. But men show no such revulsion toward their own semen, nor do they extend the reductionist reasoning to include their own daily defecation and urination as unclean animal functions. At any rate, those biological realities seem to affect male self-estimate very little.

Why do men denigrate woman, showing such distaste for some basic elements of organic sexuality?

Because they desire women so much.

Being so frequently frustrated, men rescue their own self-esteem by rationalizing their rejection by woman. "I never wanted her anyway", a man lies to himself. "She is repulsive." So it is, as a modern Aesop would tell you, that men who have failed to obtain sex from a woman explain away their failure with one woman by a self-consoling diatribe against her, against all women. The best women are subject to the worst abuse, because they are desired by many and reject many, thus multiplying the number of frustrated potential detractors.

The more intensely a man desires a woman, the more he will malign her if she proves unattainable. Men despise women whom they long for but cannot have, because male pride prevents them from acknowledging their own unworthiness and inferiority.

It is of interest to note in this context of male characterization of the female an antithesis, namely, that some men idealize and angelicize the unattainable woman, spiritualizing her sexuality until it becomes aetherial. The historical example of that is the cult of courtly love. Or we recognize it in a type of adolescent male psychology; adolescence is the period in which privation and frustration may be somewhat sweet and histrionic. Angelicizing the female is an attempt at sublimation of drive. However, chronic privation gradually loses its Romantic allure. Poets become cynics, panegyrics become misogynist bitterness.

Distorting a woman into a fantasy-image, whether more base or more pure than she actually is, results from the mourning of desire speaking in ignorance of the actual. The mis-estimated woman is the misrepresented woman.

Only intimate personal contact and tolerant love will discover the essential female person, the woman-as-she-is.

209

The beautiful that they want but cannot have:—That is what men try to make so ugly.

The unattainable is the not-worth-having;—don't you see the logic, the perverse faulty logic, of men's hostility toward women?

210

I have found the cause of a man's revulsion toward women in the experience of repeated repulsion by women. Men who have been put off by women are most avid in putting women down. Their misogyny is a perverse form of dammed-up and polarized eroticism, their antipathy the reversal of their once-great craving.

Every time a woman rejects a man, she risks creating an enemy. Yet, if a woman wants to be appreciated for herself, she must be open and receptive. That is a woman's dilemma,—how to offer herself universally without yielding herself promiscuously.

211

A young man's obscenity, the graffiti on toilet stalls, is the frustration of drive unable to express itself naturally. It is the impatient yowling of the whelp coyote.

An old man's obscenity, sex linked to scatology, is the bitter nostalgia of the impotent. The old dog growls and moans as he walks his circle before lying down.

In both cases, of course, the grudge is against woman, whether woman who withholds herself or woman who will not be satisfied by inadequate efforts. There is a further grudge being expressed by obscenity, a grudge against instinct, instinct that urges on when there are no prospects or taunts when the man has lapsed into incapacity.

Obscenity is the poisoned dish of frustration and disappointment.

The man who is fulfilled or who has been fulfilled and cherishes the memory of it has no taste for obscenity. Fulfillment has purified his attitude toward sex and toward woman. Whatever the surge or ebb of the instinct within him, he will always value the process of instinct highly, he will always value women highly.

212

A young female married teacher at the language institute where I teach received an anonymous letter from one of her students one day. She brought it in to the office and threw it on the desk with shocked indignation, as the directress and I sat discussing some academic matters.

The directress, Miss Lawrey, one of those proper British aging virgins, was baffled by the teacher's rude intrusion, until she read the first few lines of the typed letter opened upon her desk.

"Oh, my, my!," she exclaimed, with that deep-felt censoriousness the British utter in the event of any impropriety.

The teacher and Miss Lawrey blushed and clucked at each other—(I by now guessing the pornographic nature of the letter)—, the two of them passing the fluster back and forth.

The teacher flurried out of the office.

Miss Lawrey began to tear up the letter. But then she stopped, looked at me, and, reaching across the desk, handed the letter to me.

I confess that my curiosity had been aroused. I did want to somehow get hold of the letter and run off to a corner somewhere to find out what kind of outrage had been perpetrated.

But when Miss Lawrey handed the letter to me unasked, shuddering and virtually wiping her hands afterwards—as if dirt were *my* department—, I contemplated the possibility that I was being subtly insulted. I perceived some such thought process as: Dirty letter = filthy sex = a man = all men = this man here.

So, I was left holding the missive...For what? To repiece the pieces and entertain myself with some spicy reading? To perform a psychoanalysis of the writer? To undertake a criminal investigation? Or merely to grade the paper's English, since it had obviously been composed by an Italian, the syntax all backwards, the vocabulary quaint?

Well, a low insult may be the route to some high insights, who knows? After all, uninhibited expression, like a dirty letter, is much more natural and spontaneous (and therefore revelatory) than the calculated, concocted, cranked-out verbiage of professional pornographers. Might the letter contain some key to aid me in my psychologist's research? I am always avid for new clues.

And so, I have the letter, have read it repeatedly, until I now write about it. And what do I find?

Well, there may be some truth to our genteel directress's crude equivalencing of one man and all men. Or is it that impersonal, anonymous sex is the same with all men, and that what refined women fear is not any one particular aggressive male, but the awesome specter of raw instinct?

Most women do not want sex for itself. They want a soul-mate of such self-restraint that he can be courteous, considerate, deferential, indeed fastidious, I mean feminine, in his sexual behavior. Oh, woman is a tamer, and doesn't she know it too. "You may have your sex eventually," she says to man, "but only if you behave yourself, speak nice to me, and learn what love is."

Contrast that feline finickiness to male canine fornicative furor. Men do not really want a woman; they can't deal with her. They just want sex, a *lady* the obstacle to that goal, as the female is the prey.

A *lady* will condescend to give a man sex, only if the puppy licks his mistress's hand first and approaches suitably subservient, whining sweetly, and with his other tail between his legs. Because a *lady* resists any crude animalization of herself with a determined will, men generally succumb, allowing themselves to be tamed. Not only men, but women too may be sexual tyrants. Not so brazen as *Carmen*, certainly, but tyrannical nonetheless.

It is not male lust that conquers, but, rather, the female demanding love. I have often warned, "Beware of lust!" Should I now shout all the louder, "And beware of love too. After all, it conquered lust."?

But seriously now. Back to the letter:—

In reading it, the first temptation I yielded to was enjoying the little errors of expression, the ridiculously Italianate phraseology and syntax. All teachers find their amusement in students' mistakes. (One of my students, assigned to writing a thank-you letter, wrote the following: "I thank you from the bottom of my heart, and from my wife's bottom too.") Students' blunders satisfy the teacher's sense of superiority.

I could copy the entire letter into this text for line-by-line analysis, but that would be a too-tedious process. I barely have the stamina to write out my own thoughts. And, besides, *Roman Ruminations* is my private Villa of Solitude; I do not rent out pages to transients. I occasionally play host to invited guests,—D.H. Lawrence, Lucretius, Thoreau, Lao-tzu, Nietzsche, Brahms, Bernini—, but I tolerate no interlopers.

Anyway, two examples of the ludicrous in the semantics and style of the letter, to give an idea of a teacher's entertainment: The writer propositions his adored sex queen thusly: "If you are costive I shall do a good clyster." (I assume he is asking permission; ah, he's already too tamed.) He proceeds to write fanciful erotic dialogue, imagining that a British woman in the throes of ecstasy will cry out excitedly, "Braek me the arse, braek me the ovaries!" [sic]

So much for diction and rhetoric. Perhaps any attempt to say sex, whether eloquently or ineptly, is inevitably absurd.

Now, into the analysis of sex-and-psyche, shall we?

These are the themes and images I found in the letter:—

1.) <u>Corporo-idolatry</u>. There is a fascinated obsession with the body and its parts, both his and hers. Not merely *somatophilia*, that pagan body-love, this obsession is actually an intense zeal for worship, for adoration. It is an idolatrous awe, *corporo-idolatry*.

The Petronius who penned the letter proclaims his worship of body parts by listing them in litany (linked, of course, by the vividest verbs he could find in the dictionary). He repeats and re-arranges body parts in incantation, an anatomical list-making reminiscent of Walt Whitman's enthusiasm for inventory.

How woefully futile, indeed, is language to treat the subject of instinct. Words are too synthetic, too inert. Representational language fails to capture the real thing. Visual art expresses the erotic so much better, as I discovered in classical sculpture. The art directly out of the unconscious is closer to instinct out of the unconscious than is any cerebral verbal fabrication.

2.) <u>Fascination with fluids</u>. Sex flows, the epistolist perceives correctly; most of the acts he proposes are lubricated by a variety of body juices and oozings. That he joyously promises to inundate her with seed, inside and out, is the stereotypical imagery of male potent *machismo*. However, he proceeds to the details of peristalsis and defecation with happy coprophilia and suggestions of some rites that made the ancient Greeks infamous.

At this point, most of us recoil in disgust. Nonetheless, there is that undeniable mortifying fact and perennial embarrassment of the physical proximity of the organs sexual to the organs excremental. That evolutionary development has tainted sex forever, and we cannot deny and ignore it. *"Inter urinas et faeces nascimur,"* the celibate Christian Church Fathers intoned ominously. Not only born there, but find love there, too.

Our Petronius rhapsodizes on his own flow, and, where he doesn't find a complementary flow from his female into him, he adopts the excremental expedient. His itemization of body parts is not sufficient; there must be a liquid laving and loving between them.

I share none of the letter writer's coprophilic enthusiasm, so I lack empathy and whatever contribution that capacity makes to human understanding. Still, Dr. Georg Groddeck has taught me tolerance.

3.) <u>Romanticism</u>. That is precisely the word, and no other. The letter is physiology spiced with Romanticism. Nothing in the letter may be interpreted as threatening or even exploitive; it is all merely overenthusiastic, which is to say, Romantic. It is even a love-letter; in fact, the honest love-letter that underlies the other, censored love-letters that men usually send to women.

The letter lauds its recipient, and, far from menacing her in any way, promises so much,—pleasure, gratification, even fulfillment. The writer is a veritable eroto-egomaniac, in short, a Romantic. He is a burning bundle of yearning, fantasy, and frustration.

At one point in the letter, the self-control and the discipline of composing coherent sentences breaks down, and our literary wooer just spurts words. He is beside himself with...with lust? No, with Romantic self-indulgence.

4.) <u>Pathos</u>. The writer finishes his letter by signing himself. Not his name, of course. After all, he has been a naughty boy in writing such a thing and surely doesn't want his identity known. He signs himself, or symbol of his sexual self, a half-page erect phallus on a testicular pedestal, effusively spurting his potency. Petronius is Priapus. As an afterthought, he adds a little drawing of wished-for entry. (Even he discovered, apparently, that words are inadequate, so he resorted to artistic pictorialism and iconographic explicitness.)

Pathetic? Of course. Sick? Only as hunger is a sickness. Final judgment? The word *guilty* is not in my vocabulary, sorry.

The letter was a desperate outcry of need, a sort of suicide in words, or at least a step in a protracted Romantic suicide. On the brink. Now over the edge!

It *is* pathetic. The male, more than the female, is the sex-suffering animal.

213

I have long suspected that make-work is what is done by those who cannot find love. Now, after a typical day of my own labor, I wonder whether the chronic physical fatigue from labor is a daily dose of enfeeblement of the erotic instinct. My perceptions jangled, my body tired and tense, I feel disinclined toward spontaneous amorous expansiveness. I am too tired to approach to touch.

As a consequence of work mania, the most highly developed societies are peopled by a thoroughly desexualized population of functionaries, cogs in the wheel of modern technology. Desensitized by their business, by their busyness, impervious to the voluptuous warmth of their own bodies and of other bodies, they are all too weary to feel the stirrings of desire.

And so they resort to pornography.

Pornography is a desperate attempt to resuscitate lost sensual sensitivity. It is like the noxious and acrid ammonia capsules broken under the nostrils of the unconscious, or the violent open-chest heart massage given to those half-dead from a coronary, or the high-voltage electrical jolt administered to what may already be a corpse. Such artificial stimulation is an advanced form of the decadence of instinct.

The pathos of the current ubiquity of pornography is that it seems to indicate that men and women are no longer attracted to each other without an intermediation of rabid fantasy.

Pornography is the user's manual by which people become physically serviceable to one another, learning all the functional possibilities of the two body mechanisms.

I posit a paradox:—The more pornography, the less eroticism. A healthy man would not need to be propagandized into being attracted to women. Only the moribund, the last-gasp man, must resort to such desperate automanipulative stimuli.

Pornography meets the needs of the sexual zombies. "I, who feel nothing, in my desperation to feel anything, will use you for that purpose." Pornography enables frustrated automanipulators to become unscrupulous mutuomanipulators. And, worst of all, even woman has now acquired a taste for pornography.

Pornography is a horror show of sex, manufactured to re-arouse the necrotic into a semblance of sensitivity. A technological detachment from instinct, pornography is a peculiar feature of high, that is, decadent societies,—very different from the erotic fertility art of primitives, as technological inertness is different from organic instinct worshipped in awe.

Pornography is a symptom of the cerebralization of instinct. Sex has become cerebral, as D.H. Lawrence diagnosed. We think about sex, talk about sex, have it always on our minds. Spontaneous instinctual attraction has been supplanted by premeditation, by obsession and compulsion.

Pornography is *about* sex—we have nothing less than a monomania about sex—, but we are no longer capable of feeling spontaneous, elemental animal attraction. No matter. In our pornographic preoccupation, we'll go on thinking and talking and fantasizing sex to death.

Work on, world, work on. Work away at sex, a task for you like anything else, our erotic relatedness just more work to be done according to the manual. Potency to the successful....and to the survivors. Exploit all the means and methods, lay bare the functions and the mechanics. Think and plot and labor and apply yourself with tense industriousness. But understand this:—You are stranding yourselves in a desolation of inert, technological wastes, far from the life-giving current of natural instinct.

Pornography is the death-warrant, the order of execution, the obituary of *eros*.

214

The true evil of pornography is the cruelty of taunting the lonely.

Vulnerability is exploited by the pornographers, who tap into, and further provoke, the sexual soliloquies of the lonely. Despite the obtuseness of the sociologists—("No harm has been shown...")—, it must be recognized that pornographers are parasites upon sickly ones.

Filling the lack of the lonely with hallucinatory satisfaction, those charlatans make the sale, then invariably return the lonely to their loneliness.

A healthy perceptive adult sees the deception and will abhor pornography as a wicked, self-exploitive addiction. And so, pornographers direct their marketing towards the ailing, or toward adolescents, the needing unwary whose intense sexual longing makes them most vulnerable of all.

Damn the pornographers, who, under the guise of proffered satisfaction, vampirize those made desperate by need!

215

The portrayal of decadence, as in books and so-called art films that pretentiously claim to show us *as we really are*, that contemporary genre of pandering voyeurism is—what else?—another form of decadence. Art is always self-revelation, those who depict decadence, decadents themselves, seem to forget.

The aesthetic theorists of former centuries who eulogized art as edification would be disconcerted to find themselves in judgment upon the culture of our time. Now art wallows. It is corruption's corruption.

Art may *put the mirror to life,* but the mirror itself is filthy.

As the producers are participants in what they portray, so the critics are deluded fools. They gaze stupidly at the smudged reflection and observe inanely, "Yes, that's me, all right." So runs the typical dictum of the literary and film critics. They offer a blessing upon the decadence.

Given our pornographic culture, a new inverse valuation must emerge:—Because art is now anti-humane, so pro-humane must be anti-art. Now, there's a state of affairs that would shock the Muses.

Self-respect now requires artlessness. Avoid contamination!

216

Nihilism has gone surreptitious. It is now in masquerade and uses the alias, *art.*

People have lost the critical faculty by which everything should be judged—self-defensively—according to humane values. That moral sense has been replaced by a willy-nilly aestheticism in which technique is supposed to cover a multitude of sins, even a criminality. We live in an age in which valuation is based upon some cliché canons of art that the hoodwinked chatter at one another. *High art* is their *summum bonum.* But how inhumane are those smug, self-deceiving aesthetes.

To give a specific example. I recently overheard some tourist young women talking about *Last Tango in Paris*, a film that I myself, lured by a cover story in *Time* magazine, had the misfortune to see in a Roman cinema. That film is a perverse and nihilistic piece of sodomy and cruelty. The innocents disbelieved their own senses and healthy instinct. They had some words of approbation for the artistic exposition of two people humiliating each other. "The sex wasn't as bad as I had heard," one pimply and pleading virgin commented irrelevantly, "and it was necessary to the story". As if that inanity could justify anything. Let the story justify itself. The other naïve dupes nodded at each other around the table in a ridiculous affirmation of the cliché.

It is not only adolescents who think and valuate like that. Indifference toward, and tolerance of cruelty may be taken as a certain sign of triumphant nihilism and a well-advanced inhumanity.

Sadism is now sacramental, if only it is depicted in an *artistic* fashion. The sex-of-death is as good as the sex-of-Life, as long as the rape and murder are splendidly staged. Appearance is valued over substance, and bullshit on art is delectable ambrosia. And we genuflect to the icons of our cruelty.

The perverse fantasy and the gross lie,—that is what art and the rationale for art have become in our day. Art was once the *imitation of Nature*. Evil ambition has taken hold of it; art is now an assault upon Nature.

We live in a moral malaise, in which everything is transmuted into its opposite. *Good* and *evil* are obsolete words, replaced now by notions of a competent, or an incompetent, aesthetic. Is there no one with insight and instinct sound enough to expose and indict the vicious hoax?

It has come to this:—The animals are all extinct; only the beasts survive.

217

If, in considering all aspects of instinct, we were to write a history of the sexes, the most significant events in that history would be the triumph of the male and the subsequent corruption of the female. It happened like this:—

Somehow, sometime in the distant past, the natural complementarity, as well as the harmonious check-and-balance between the sexes, was disrupted. Male willful assertiveness came to predominate over female earth-belonging.

The human female's hold over the human male was once powerful—he first worshipped mother-goddesses, remember—, but with advances in male megalomania through the development of the male mind the female's hold loosened. His own sex pulled up into his head, the male transformed his eroticism into a self-obsession with his own sexual power mystique.

When the male mind launched its campaign against the female, a chronic estrangement between the sexes set in. The male asserted his force of body and mind against the female. At first she resisted, countering his aggression with her allure, ever more feebly, until at last she was left to trail behind her now all-conquering master. Patriarchalism dethroned the mother-goddess.

Where once there was mutual need and help, now the relatedness between the sexes was infected by power and subjugation. Mating and bonding became an exercise of male dominance over the female.

Coitus between the victor male and the subjugated female was no longer the sex-of-instinct. The sex-of-instinct is deep organic communion, selfless immersion into the flow of Life Itself. In sex, the male must yield; but he would not, he was too willful. And so, coitus lost its instinctual essence, the return to earth and to the current of Life. The wholesome animal sanity that can be found only in instinct was lost to both man and woman.

A consequence of the triumph of the male was the gradual corruption of the female. Sensing that her own sexual sway over man had diminished and become futile, the woman turned to mimicking man and emulating his behavior. If she could not be mate and complement to him, she would identify herself with him, become like him, and, in that way, find some accommodation. In our time, we witness the final stage in the process, namely, the emergence of woman as pseudo-male. (The Roman satirist Juvenal was outraged by the idea of female gladiators. Well, we can show him female boxers, female wrestlers, and female soldiers. Cinematic fantasies now portray the female as warlike as the male.)

Evidence of the corruption of woman is her mindfulness of sex, imitative of the male. She too has got her sex into her head, as D.H. Lawrence was the first to recognize. Just like the male, woman has become self- and sex-conscious. Primordial female sexuality had been mind-less, instinctual, visceral, tellurian, a spontaneous energetic of the animal unconscious. Modern woman has abandoned both her instincts and her intuition to take up male willfulness. Woman has lost herself.

Human sexuality has become male-erotic, that is, characterized by manipulation, exploitation, the compulsion-to-control and the compulsion-to-repeat. Woman has learned the lesson of her defeat. She too has become predatory.

Sexuality seems inconceivable apart from the dynamic harmony and complementarity between male and female, the *yin-yang* of healthy relatedness. Yet, modern man and woman are both empty husks of denatured animality. What we now have is a bizarre mock-sexuality between two masculinized sexes, the female too now a muscle-pumper. And when the natural female was corrupted, the sex-of-instinct was extinguished; it may now be a fossil dynamic.

What are we left with, then? In the human, sex was reduced from an all-pervading instinct to a psychological power-play and merely physical drive, from prime energetic to episodic act, from a controlling force to a controlled one. Sex was turned into an *it*.

The male has vanquished the female and corrupted her with the worst traits of his own sex. That is the history of the sexes in a sentence.

218

The American woman has at last become enthusiastic. And about what? Her own sexual satisfaction.

Woman has learned self-gratification from man, and she loves it. She considers her own body a tool to serve her private gratification.

Man has nothing to fear from that development. He will, in fact, feel less estranged from woman, when he discovers that she now thinks and behaves just like him. The sexes have something in common, at last. Man need only strike the bargain of reciprocal manipulation and do his duty toward woman.

Man need not fear, but Life is in terror at what is happening to woman. Modern woman considers the life-process within her a sexist curse; she is as averse to fertility and nurturance as she is enamored of her self-gratification. Selfish, self-seeking, the new masculinized woman. This is the dawn of an era of unprecedented female pathology.

Woman doesn't recognize her derangement, nor will man tell her that she has contracted his own worst. I have encountered the modern woman, and I am alarmed. Woman is sick. Who, then, will look after Life? Who can assume woman's sacred responsibility? Life is too precious to be entrusted to the pathological whims of the modern woman.

219

The American feminist movement, *women's liberation* as it is grandiloquently called, is a symptomatic ideological development of our time.

Sorry to stoop to *ad feminam* argument, but no other contemporary social movement is so reducible to the pathologies of its leaders as is this shrill assemblage of viragoes, lesbians, and cerebral shrews. They are the modern Amazons who cut off their breasts in order to better wield battleaxes against the men.

Women's liberation confesses a bankruptcy of the feminine and a deep disturbance of female sexuality, a transvestitism of identity. It is the culmination, the success, of the male's historical campaign to corrupt the female. Unfortunately for the male, the female is exercising her recently learned will-to-power against him.

Should we acknowledge, along with Nietzsche, that "There is little of man here; therefore, their women strive to be mannish"? That may be, but, even so, separate pathologies may explain, but they do not justify one another.

The feminists want the American woman to be absolutely equal to man...a step down. The sameness of the sexes as envisioned by the women's liberationists is unnatural and impossible. Despite the rationalizing rhetoric that they intend equalization only in the economic and political realms, in actuality they strike at the natural psycho-physiological duality. They can't stand duality, but they want adversarial polarization, matriarchal revolution against the old patriarchalism. (The *arch* root in those two words means *to rule over*.)

If woman harbors a festering grudge, let her not name it *social progress*. Harmony between the sexes is to be achieved only by dynamic complementarity, not by gender warfare.

Women's liberationists, you self-styled enlightened reformers, you are uncomprehending when it comes to organic wisdom. In apeing man, you have lost femininity and womanhood. Unfortunate, misguided plotters, what you are attempting is unattainable, except through destruction of humanness.

The worst public enemies are those who fan the flames of hostility between the sexes.

220

The prostitute lies love when she lies down to love. Feigning fulfillment of the male's fantasies, she is an unyielding yielder, an intimate who is far away, a frigid fire, an armored nude, a no-thinking yes-doer. Her apparent acceptance of the man masks a profound rejection. The prostitute is never truly got into when she is got onto.

Whoring is lying lying. It is false sex, false passion, false love...fornication as fraud.

221

The most immoral kind of woman is one who feigns feelings.

The most immoral kind of man is one who has no feelings.

222

Living here in Rome makes me think of the prostitute and the priest, two types I observed during some of the very first scenes of my Roman solitude.

The prostitute exploits one of man's physiological vulnerabilities, the need for sex, and for doing that she is consigned to the role of detested social parasite. The priest exploits one of man's psychological vulnerabilities, the fear of death; for doing that he is honored as a model and oracle of human morality.

When we are vulnerable, when we succumb to our weaknesses, then do the charlatans descend upon us with their fraudulent therapies. Beckoning to bed, the prostitute offers pretended passion, love, and personal acceptance. Inviting approach to the coffin, the priest purveys death-overcoming resurrection and salvation. A momentary orgasm or eternal bliss,—problem solved!

Man the needing, man the fearful, stretches out a hand to each of his seducers in a piteous plea for help. The prostitute smiles as she takes his hand and draws him down to satisfy him. The priest beams reassuringly as he bends in blessing to deliver him. And man is drawn and tortured on the rack, fettered in lifelong bondage to desire and to dread.

The prostitute is a love-liar, the priest a death-dealer. Do those two classes perceive the affinity in their vocations, in their predations? They do recognize each other's power, they do detest each other's influence. But the priest has cut himself a better portion of the carcass. Man's ebbing animality is making him numb to instinct, while his increasing cerebrality is making him ever more susceptible to metaphysical anxiety.

I once heard about a prostitute who confessed that she had let herself be bedded by an out-of-uniform priest. Unknowingly, she had done it. When, later, she found out who and what he was, she was horrified at the enormity. For the first time she felt sinful. She, a seducer, had been seduced by her adversary, her judge. The prostitute must yield to the priest, for she too must one day die and face divine judgment.

The priest will win out. We will abandon instinct to save our souls.

In her deception, the prostitute at least provides something, but that little illusion is attacked by the priest, who hurls the epithet *Mortal Sin!* against it. The priest, devotee of death, is ever at war with Life, and so sex too is his enemy. Himself a total abstainer, he attempts to regulate sex in others, curb sex, condemn it, do anything to prevent sex from returning us to Life. Who would attend the Requiem, if the joys of Dionysian revelries streamed through into our human lives?

If a man is convinced to curse sex, the priest pronounces him about to be redeemed. If a man curses Life and this earth, the priest exults, "You are saved! Now you will live forever!" Then the sufferer turns away from the prostitute toward the priest and abandons himself to life renunciation.

The priest touches him with the clammy hand of grace. Another victory of heaven over earth, of salvation over sex, of death over Life. A soul has been saved! Tightening the rack into which he has secured the man, the priest promises to stay near to ease the convert's suffering, to make it meaningful and salvific, to make suffering more gratifying than sex ever was.

The prostitute is an honest hypocrite compared to the priest; her deceit is a game, as everyone knows before playing. The priest, however, is presumptuous enough to pretend to divine truth and metaphysical potency.

For her open naïveté the prostitute is condemned. For his incredibly elaborate craft, the priest is venerated. But how can we ever compare the petty mischief of the sisters of sex to the deeply cruel deception and exploitation perpetrated by the pimps of death?

223

Celibacy would be as achievable as any other self-discipline, if it weren't for one insuperable objection, namely, an attractive woman. Given a world in which all females were as censorious as schoolmarms, as desiccate as nuns, or as antipathetic as feminists, then celibacy and self-denial would be a happy practice. Alas, women, and especially these Italian women around me, are not like that.

I walk through the streets of Rome, and the women I pass make the celibacy discipline seem the most inhuman estrangement and worst possible personal curse. I blink, I sigh, I seethe, I swell, I sizzle.

It takes only one beautiful woman's being to inadvertently but absolutely refute the entire elaborated rationale of the celibacy cult. Spontaneous appreciation returns us to life-loving good sense. Reality renders every ideology ridiculous.

Why persist in suffocating ourselves, when a deep breath is so invigorating?

Let us not into titillation. But deliver us from celibacy. Amen.

224

(Watching the new priests kneeling in the ceremony of ordination, as the Pope inducts them:—)

A vow of celibacy is analogous to a vow of perpetual silence. Except for the Tao or Nature or the All, an unrelated ONE is impossible.

It is ruinous futility to attempt to become sufficient unto oneself. Only diminution and impoverishment can result from such resolution, whether to be celibate or silent. Can a man who is apart, who is muffled and mute, become, in any way, better? Is spirituality to be identified with the unnatural?

These men will live their lives as an unending Lent. A little of life is lost each day in which a man languishes in privation or in the silent soliloquy of his own barren thoughts.

Extra alium nulla salus:—My prescription for salvation.

225

St. Paul wrote, "It is better to marry than to burn."

For that prescription, I hope that St. Paul is burning, on top of the pyre of his pernicious epistles.

226

The most exquisitely gratifying of self-indulgences is the self-denial of all gratification. In the matter of extremes, the ascetics are the most accomplished libertines.

227

The formula, "Familiarity breeds contempt", is probably to be understood in the context of Puritanical propaganda against sex. The Calvinists were very adroit in attempting to prove by dogma that satisfaction is immoral, that even human love is damnable.

From my own life experience, I would say that "Familiarity engenders empathy". I am contemptuous only of what I am detached from; with deepening intimacy I feel a kinship and warm sympathy for persons.

I love a woman for her visceral animality, her body with both its *higher* and *lower* aspects. She is like me in her humanness. I feel no contempt for the nature and processes that we share.

Wholesome love is that for the physical and the present; any love for the abstract and the absent (e.g, even for *God*) is unwholesome.

"Familiarity breeds contempt"? I wonder whether the Calvinists were consistent in their belief in that saying and would thus start each day by spitting into their mirrors.

228

I was once a reluctant participant at a bachelor party, where a mob of men had assembled for a ritualistic farewell to one of them who was to be married soon.

Everyone got rowdy and liquored up. The theme of the occasion seemed to be the word *fuck*, which was bandied about in coarse jokes and apprehensive assaults upon the institution of marriage. The gathering reeked of drunkenness, adolescent group homoeroticism, and male tribalism.

The good spirits roused up were like those when one is whistling in the dark in the deep, frightening wood. After all, Marriage the Monster lurked ahead. There was even a gladiatorial mockshow, as everyone urged the prospective groom on, encouraging with the hollow praise that he was a better man than the institutional adversary he was about to face.

What cowards men are. It took twelve of his fellows to embolden the man to venture into intimacy with his new wife. Philanderers, afraid of women.

Meanwhile, back at the bride's family home, she must have been sitting and wondering what he was up to that night. Suspicion and estrangement already. Poor girl, she'll have to face it alone. It seems that it is the stags, rather than the does that herd up for protection.

I couldn't determine whether the bachelor party was a sacrilegious rite-of-passage or a mock requiem. In any case, it was full of puerilism and bad taste. What a way to start a marriage.

229

A married man I know recently told me that he was "sexually frustrated". Well, I suppose that his wife must have her monthly periods, and she has three of his children to care for, so she cannot always be at her husband's instinctual beck-and-call.

"Sexually frustrated". Imagine. The petty complaint of someone who endures a day of fast made to a lone, delirious desert-soul about to die of starvation.

Better an occasional meager meal than none at all. Marriage looks succulent to the single.

230

I read in the *Rome Daily American* this morning that there were nine hundred thousand divorces in the United States last year. That means one million eight hundred thousand men and women failed in committed love and several million children become half-orphaned. At such an annual rate of divorce and with so many children affected, how far in the future are the extinction of the American family and the consequent disintegration of American society?

Why are the Americans so badly mated? How can we account for the ominous multiplication of divorces?

If God ever blessed America, He showered it with material resources, not with wisdom and happiness. In all my travels, I have never encountered a people so favored but so discontented. Land of wealth and of *enlightened* education, of the highest standard of living and the lowest standard of loving, America is a huge emotional muddle.

Having apparently lost their guiding instincts, the Americans gorge themselves on psychological knowledge, but they show little psychological wisdom. They live in an ambivalence somewhere between scientific sex education and cruel pornography. They teach sex, but they do not learn love. They learn sex, but they do not show love. They may succeed in sex, but they fail in love.

There is a generational momentum in the social disintegration. Children of lost love and failed families repeat their parents' experience, and their children repeat it again, until more and more of them pass their lifetimes in emotional shocks and privations. Each generation compounds the catastrophe, and the society as a whole withers.

That is what is happening in America. The crisis is obvious to even them. But what do the Americans prescribe for themselves as a cure? Why, sex therapy, or, more precisely, fornicative know-how. Tragic stupidity. As usual, an epidemic is followed by a plague of quack healers.

In the American environment of "free, open, honest, candid discussion of sex" and "liberation from ignorance, inhibition, and Puritanism", in that aura of hedonistic democracy and scientific cunning, what happens?

Couples uncouple.

Nine hundred thousand annual uncouplings hardly constitute a victory for American sexual *liberation*. But how the Americans love their methodology of manipulation! The genitals are, in any case, easier to direct than the heart and mind. And so much easier to teach our children what to do than what responsibility entails. Yes, sex is a simpler concept than love, individual liberty and license more attractive than lifetime commitment.

With their bizarre fusion of psychoscience and Romanticism, the Americans are abusing themselves, one another, and their children.

I used to wander the streets in that Land of the Lost, I myself an orphan among the orphans. The one million eight hundred thousand and more hurried around me, all lonely and withdrawn into their bitter selves.

The Americans long for love, but they cannot forget or overcome their losses, their inadequacies, and their failures.

231

A lonely bachelor's rejoinder to the unfaithful married man who offers him advice on the methods for the pursuit of women:

"I am sorry that I lack the skill you have shown in getting that which you no longer want."

232

The assurance that there is a woman-already-won waiting for him at home gives a man the restless urge to cheat on his wife.

Her taken-for-granted fidelity provokes his infidelity.

233

Marital infidelity is the most cruel, the most deeply hurting offense that one person can commit against another. Of all the Shakespeare plays, I have understood *Othello* the best, I have felt it most.

Marriage is a promise that evokes trust. He promises her fidelity, she believes his promise, she puts her trust in him. She promises him fidelity, he believes her promise, he puts his trust in her. That is what marriage is,—the promise and trust.

When the promise is disregarded and broken, when the self-indulgence of sexual infidelity is sought out, the other person, trusting spouse, feeling duped and betrayed, suffers that deep, most personal hurt and repudiation.

What strays in adultery is not the body or the genitals, but the commitment of the mind and the reckless assertion of will. The mind contradicts the *yes* of marriage with a cruel *no*; the will asserts *I* against *we*. Adultery is the worst treachery against the other, and it is virtually unforgivable.

If the adultery is kept secret, the offender lives in the hypocrisy of pretended keeping-of-the-promise, fraudulent meriting of the trust. If the adultery is confessed, the hidden act becomes the direct spoken insult; the trust of the other is exposed to ridicule. Worst of all is the stubborn infidelity that confesses no mere onetime lapse, but with a determined will continues in the adultery in spite of the promise. That last, once discovered, is the most horrible rejection of the faithful spouse, almost a nullification of the other: "You are nothing to me anymore. You are nothing."

After exposure of adultery, life-mates to each other no longer, the couple become the guilty one and the aggrieved one. The estrangement caused by sexual infidelity becomes self-destructive willfulness in the one who was unfaithful and self-torturing bitterness in the one who was betrayed.

When adultery breaks a marriage, the children too are its victims. Another promise—that of full father-and-mother parental nurturance of the children—is broken. Looking into the faces of the children, the aggrieved custodial parent sees the likeness of the treacherous former spouse; how can she or he look at those faces without unconscious loathing?

The grief and bitterness of the one betrayed is directed into hatred of the other, (perhaps of all others of that gender), hatred of sex, hatred of marriage itself. Skeptical of all promises, of all trust, the aggrieved one cannot get over the experience. The lesson he or she learns is that promises are not kept, that the other gender is treacherous, that trust is foolish. Then that person becomes incapacitated for love and committed relatedness. What worse harm could be done to another person than to incapacitate him or her for love and relatedness?

The betrayed spouse may even be driven to thoughts of murder, as in *Othello*, and to thoughts of suicide too. If the verdict is blame-the-other, the sentence may be murder; if the verdict is blame-oneself, then suicide. Whether either judgment, love and sex have led to premature death. For what is life worth without promises and trust, love and relatedness?

The social consequence of general acceptance of promiscuous adultery is the extinction of marriage. The adulteries of others, along with divorces, are taken by innocent singles as cautionary lessons. Demoralized by the broken marriages they witness, the unmarried shy away from making a promise, from believing a promise, from trusting trust. Anticipating adultery, failure, humiliation, divorce, they do not marry. They indulge in sex, they attempt episodic sex liaisons, but only with standoffish relatedness, their love ever tentative and provisional. They may even live together in a masquerade of marriage. But first and foremost they think of self-protection. The cautionary examples of those many who have not restrained themselves induce others to withhold themselves.

Because of adultery, as because of divorce, marriage has become frightening. To the observant young, marriage looks like the potential ruination of their selves, their lives, and their souls.

234

The male is predatory.

The spider lies awaiting in his lair of lust, eyes all wide and gleaming, fangs drooling, set to pounce. He crouches, lurking with claw tips sensing the strands in his web of devious charm. He has spun with seductive words and alluring gestures the gossamer weave of his snare of lechery. Now he waits panting, his hairy body bristling in the impatient tension of arousal.

A delicate fair-winged form flies amiss and falls headlong into the sticky weave of the web. She struggles in her entrapment, only to be entrapped still more. Her wings, whirring in panic and futility, entangle her deep in the web.

The spider reacts, feeling in the taut strands the victim's helpless flapping. He leaps out of his lair and runs toward the trapped one with a hot frenzy to devour.

In an instant he stands above her, looming and striking terror with his glowing eyes. He savors his power over the defenseless one beneath him.

He spreads his body over her, his legs caging her fitful struggle.

She is still a moment. Has terror killed her?

He lowers himself to her, fangs pulsing, voracious in desire.

Suddenly, the shock!

Uncoiling in an explosion, she arches her body and raises her sprung stinger, furiously buzzing, stabbing and stabbing, ferociously fighting.

The two bodies tumble and struggle in a frenzied death-match of fang against stinger. Spurts of blood splotch the rumpled sheet of the web, as they clutch and bite and sting each other.

Then, one falls, lapsing with spasms into the woven shroud.

The other, grievously wounded, staggers away in victor's agony.

The male is predatory.

But woe to him on the day that the spider unknowingly traps, and tangles with, a wasp!

235

Many of us learn the bitter lesson that self-seeking sex corrupts the generous self-giving of love relationships. *Libido* assaults *eros*. If the lover no longer serves to do to us that which we want done to us, then the lover is loved no longer. The one who doesn't meet our needs is needed no more.

The genitals usurp the place of the heart, and the heart defers. And the female, the modern decadent female, has become as sexually exploitive as the male. Hasn't the female learned her lesson in predatoriness from the way man has long treated her? Isn't there a new breed of sexual harpies who grapple with the satyrs in a competition for autogratification? Both sexes are now on the prowl to lure innocents looking for love into the snare of self-seeking sex.

How much hurt we inflict in the compulsive quest for gratification irrespective of the other!

The dominant value in our contemporary society is that of *use*. The grasping, acquisitive tentacles of use extend themselves through all our lives, even into the sacred shrine of the other person. After the lover is used, abused, used up until useless, then he or she is disposed of, as just so much emotional rubbish.

We plunder the world and one another. Many are the casualties of our predations. The exploited learn to exploit in turn, and a justification, a rationale, even a mystique of exploitation is elaborated. One guise of our greed we cynically call *love*.

Eros turns away and weeps...for us.

236

The intent of my dreams lately seems to be to provide a symbolic postscript to my daily thoughts.

In the predawn hours of this Sunday morning, I returned to Brazil (in my mind, land of *eros*). The rich complexity of the dream narrative is not completely intelligible, my unconscious apparently determined to assert more than it would reveal. However, I do understand two brief scenes as a commentary upon some of my recent ruminations:

I approached the ticket girl at the theater in Penedo, and, after some brief dialogue, went inside the booth with her. She took my hand and clasped it. (The females in erotic dreams are unfailingly responsive.) In a few moments, after a bit of breathy whispering, I passed my hand along her warm thigh. How so direct and forthright is *libido*!

The girl disappeared abruptly, leaving me in the booth alone. I felt a mild, fleeting guilt at my indecent advances so soon after acquaintance and therefore impersonal.

In the second scene of the dream, I accompanied the theater owner (the girl's father) to the house to see her. The two of us climbed to the roof, as I made pleasant conversation to ingratiate myself with the father and so further my designs upon the girl. Removing a clay roof tile, the father glared lecherously down into the lit interior of his house. The man's perversion suddenly shocked me. He indicated that my desires would be satisfied. Was his daughter naked and helpless inside?

The two of us then descended through a small hole made by removing a few more roof tiles. Touching down on the floor, the father walked into another room, and I followed.

And there his daughter lay, nude, half-uncovered on a large bed. I approached her.

"Look at what he has done!", she cried out.

She rolled over to reveal wicked welts on her bared back, her fair skin lashed and shredded.

"Who did that to you?", I asked.

She may have replied, her father, or her brother, or perhaps her answer to me was "Everyman".

I leaned forward and tenderly cradled her head in my arms to comfort and console her. I stroked her hair softly, kissing her lightly on the forehead, chastely upon her eyelid.

Then my kisses descended along her face to the allurement of her lips, and my hand grasped her bare breast as I slid down into bed beside her. . .

What allegory was that dream, with its mingling of the elements of lust and love, and I myself cast as villain? How am I to regard myself as representative of man, I who sinned, then felt a redemptive compassion, only to sin again? My dream was a *tu quoque* against myself.

The bed and the punished woman. The bed, arena of love, infirmary for the ailing, threshold to the grave. It is there, in bed, that we lie down to love and to death, to love together, to death alone. And the punished woman, punished by man in a bed, sexually punished, the beauty of her body disfigured by violence. Woman as slave, as prostitute, as victim. Male sexuality as exploitive, sadistic, cruel, death dealing:—Those were the themes of my dream.

A woman suffers in the preservation of her sexual purity and suffers in the loss of it. Her inadvertent seductive attractiveness beckons man to come to hurt her.

Aren't these all melancholy images and musings? My awake mind composes weak abstractions, but my unconscious in a dream most vividly portrays the human tragedy.

237

Modern men and women are bored. What else is there to do but abuse one another?

At the pharmacy across the street from the *pensione* in which I live, there is attached to a post along the sidewalk a large, gray metallic machine that dispenses prophylactics, curbside service for those too timid to enter the pharmacy to request from another human being such a discreet item. Or perhaps the machine is meant for the convenience of after-hours' service, when, in any case, the offered product is generally put to use.

A remarkable example of the output of the *Deutsche Gessellschaaft*, the machine gives its instructions in German, thus bewildering two Roman girls and a rotund boy—(or was it a midget?)—who, in passing by, stopped, then ambled away from such an exorbitant price for chewing gum.

There are actually three types of condom offered, each remarkably effective in its insulating qualities, but priced differently in what must be an appeal to the traditional European class consciousness.

Let there be separation in our intimacies. We will get attached with detachment. Passion will be sheathed.

The union with an interposed barrier, whether physical or psychological—that calculating sexual adventurism—pulls apart, rather than brings together. Mocking the desperation of the separate, isolated sexual climaxes of the estranged man and woman the condom lies, between.

It seems to me that the heart and mind of man and woman have also become condomized.

238

Her love said, "This is for you, as I am for you."

His lust answered, "I use you to do it to myself."

239

The usual pattern of human sexual relatedness is not timid touch deepening into transcendent intimacy, but, rather, precipitous orgasm trailing away into bitter aftermath. Not a crescendo, but a bang. Not incandescence, but fizzle-out.

240

The modern person, the manipulator, has become shallow. No longer capable of feeling lonely. No longer capable of feeling shy. And even the mystery of sex has become vulgar small talk.

241

The occurrence of sexual perversion is to be attributed to a chronic disturbance of the economics of animal energy. Perversion is an anguished expression of frustration at the lack of opportunity to discharge ever-flowing erotic energy in a normal animal way. If outlet is barricaded, a person will suffer an emotional cataclysm, whether explosion (sadism) or implosion (masochism).

One who lacks a sexual relationship—the solitary, celibate, widowed—, one who is not wholesomely mated to a lover, is especially susceptible to episodes of perverse behavior or to full chronic perversion. That susceptibility is rooted in lack; it subsists irrespective of a person's *character* or past normal adjustment.

We are creatures of circumstance and happenstance. The type and model of the ever-moral man hermetic in his inviolable integrity is a myth. Everyone is susceptible to being corrupted. We are all susceptible, as long as we remain alive.

Unfortunately, we cannot stockpile satisfactions to tide us over periods of privation; their only residue is in memory. Recollection stimulates imagination, making privation even more difficult to endure. A man who loses love sometimes loses his good self.

I must contradict a friend of mine who mischievously offered the definition that "Virtue is lack of opportunity". It is, rather, vice that results from lack of opportunity. Depraved is deprived.

There is a mingling of sound and sense between the words *perversion* and *privation.*

The sane satisfaction of normal human need is a security against behavioral perversion, against vice. The instinct of *eros* leads all toward a healthy sexual relationship. Given an opportunity, all human beings could develop a loving sexual normality, free from the desperate, compulsive reaction to frustration and privation that is perversion.

242

As for behavior, so for the person. The most cogent rebuttal I can think of to the indictment, "He is only a..." is the objection, "But he hasn't had the opportunity to be..."

The kept-from and the taken-away are insidious corruptors of us all.

Every malicious extreme is a symptom of a terrible deprivation of the fullness of life; all derangement is a desperate attempt at remedy for privation. It is not the bad he *is*, but the good he has never had or the good that he has lost that accounts for what he has become.

Once we understand that the worst is only the most impoverished, we no longer condemn. Let us be generous, let us fill the lack. There is no one so evil but that there lacks only that other person to draw out of him a healthy, moral human being.

I hate the detached judgmentalism of our traditional morality. Let us smash the *old tablets* of moral absolutes and try to acquire some sympathetic human understanding.

243

What is it, then, that is lacking? Why, participation, partaking of, being a part of, belonging. Aren't these the words of the sage?:—"Need is the instinct toward belonging."

Perversion? No, privation. The voyeurs only look to see themselves, crave to see themselves, in what they are looking at. They want to participate, to belong.

The worst in us:—That is due to our being isolated and excluded.

244

I say again, to understand human perversity you must understand human privation. There is a loneliness physiological as well as a loneliness psychological. Become an expert on loneliness, and you will then understand the all of psychology.

We are *evil* only because of what we lack. Our redemption, then, is not to be attained by ecclesiastical absolution and a return to more lack. As it is being-apart that causes perversion, so the return to health must come from the effort to become a part of.

I substitute the image of a *singula damnata* for St. Augustine's misanthropic *massa damnata*, that pathological view of man espoused by our religion. If we want to belong to the elect, we must re-integrate into human relatedness. Redemption is the fruit of inclusion. To become moral, become more-all.

245

During the course of the long Roman itinerary I conducted from primordial cell to psychoanalysis, I provoked to moral valuations, first of instinct, then of intellect. But what about the valuation of morality itself? What do you think of our morality? Is it the best possible one? Are you satisfied with it?

I wouldn't expect you to find our morality immoral—even I am too conventional in my thinking to go that far—, but does our morality succeed in its goals, which I take to be the ennobling of the individual and the equity and harmony of social relations?

Our morality is the *old tablets* that we acquired in antiquity, the enumerated commandments engraved on stone, along with a few philosophers' dicta thrown in as a secular component. Our morality is oracular, therefore authoritatively true and absolute. There are the divine laws, there is the command to conformity to those laws, and there is threatened punishment for violation.

As for the content of the moral laws, the laws-in-themselves,—that does nothing toward the ennoblement of the individual. The stuff of the moral code is just precepts. Precepts have nothing to do with character. It is not in the code, but in conformity to, obedience to, the code that, in religious morality, the individual is supposed to be ennobled; high morality is a punctilious obedience to the divine directives. But that begins to sound like a trained dog's morality.

If character is supposed to be affected by obedience, it is also affected by disobedience, by *sin*. Now, since the main enforcer of the religious moral code is the individual oneself, through the cultivated faculty of *conscience*, our morality is thoroughly psychologized. I measure myself against the standards set by the Sinai oracle. I scrutinize myself, I judge myself.

What happens to my self-estimate, as conscience exercises its lifelong surveillance? Because of our resident conscience and our memories, what we have done determines what we come to think of ourselves, then what we think of ourselves determines what we do, and so on, in reciprocal relation, a helix-spiral upward or downward. The usual outcome of the interplay between deeds and self-estimate is a thorough demoralization.

Ennobled by our morality? Who is ennobled by guilt? Who arrives at old age with even a shred of self-respect remaining?

So much for the illusion of ennoblement through morality. (St. Augustine and the other theologians did tell us from the very beginning that we are sinners.)

The second goal of morality, that of regulating social interactions, might belong better to civil and criminal law, worked out by human reason, than to any oracle. We have the history of the development of law by the ancient Romans to provide us with a model of human self-sufficiency to regulate social relations, even on a universal scale.

The Roman judges could order violent criminals beheaded, crucified, or fed to the beasts. We seem always to have believed that there is no effective law without the threat of dire punishments. There have been some dissenters—"Beware of those in whom the desire to punish is strong," Nietzsche warned; but those were eccentric voices. Punishment has been deemed indispensable, as deterrent, or, that failing, as retribution.

The law may resort to capital punishment, a quick end to the offender. Religious morality, unlimited in its means, has asserted the most dire of all threatened punishments, namely, eternal agony, *Hell*, the capital punishment that never ends. A more fearsome threat, certainly, but a deterrent only to the true-believers, who, if they are indeed true believers, obey the commandments without threats; obey in order to please God, in order not to commit an *offense against God.*

Both criminal law and religious morality are dogmatic on the notion of *free will*, along with its consequent, culpability. *Free will* is a fine justification that enables the judges to feel righteous as they remove the troublemakers from among us.

One wonders what would have happened if we had never received the divine revelation, the oracle of religious morality, if we had just worked out our own moral and ethical code on the basis of consensus and good old-Roman practicality, a utilitarian morality with no pretensions to metaphysical authority.

In that case, there would be no *sin*, even if there would be wrongs and crimes. There would be no *conscience*, although the legal system would make it clear to the offender what he had done wrong. Without *sin* or *conscience*, self-estimate would not be poisoned by oneself. Punishment would remain, as necessary, but, without *Hell*, there would be no free-floating anxiety to afflict. A depsychologized morality,—think of it!

Ennoblement of the individual would be more achievable, I think, without the withering self-scrutiny, self-indictment, and anxiety about eternal damnation. Religious morality does not make moral, so much as it hobbles and cowers. It makes us abject. "Blessed are the poor in spirit." "Fear of God".

When one considers the historical record of the anarchic Christian regime of the Middle Ages against its predecessor, the secular law and order of the Roman Empire, the effectiveness of religious morality in regulating social relations is cast into dark doubt.

The message inculcated by religious morality is: "I am a sinner. I deserve to suffer and die and then be punished." The message of our civil and criminal law is: "If I want to get along, I'd better go along." The latter seems to me a more productive approach. It commits no assault upon my self-respect. Its threat of punishment, although real, is only implicit and proportionate.

I have come to doubt whether our religious morality has made a single person better—the good ones might just adopt religious belief as an ideology congenial to their temperament and inclinations—or prevented a single crime.

What is our traditional morality? To me it seems a reign of psychological subversion and intimidation.

Now, what do *you* think about our traditional morality?

Interlude: "The Shroud"

[An autobioscene in a Roman restaurant]

"Normano Romano!"

"*Dottóre!*", I answered. Even without having seen who it was who addressed me, I knew who it had to be.

"Gianandrea! I thought you were gone off to Milano."

"Milano, *sì*, Normano, and Torino too. But, as you can see, I am back. Here I am, *ritornato a Roma!*"

I was sitting alone at one of the two outside tables at Vincenzo's, near the Porta Pia.

"And you, what are you doing here now?", Gianandrea asked me. "*Sólo, sénza una bèlla signorina.*"

"I'm doing what I always do. Brooding over the cultural problems of Rome."

"*Brooding?* Does that word mean thinking hard and feeling bad? In our city of *la dolce vita*? Only an American would do that. Are you a Protestant?"

"No. A skeptic."

"Skeptic? *Fuòri da* Roma! Go home, Yankee. Roma is no place for skeptics. What do you want to do, eh? Empty the city of the *pellegrini* and tourists and make the *Romani* have to do some honest work for a living?"

"The pilgrims will always come to Rome, Gianandrea. Nothing I think or say or write will discourage them...Where are you on your way to? How about joining me in a glass of Frascati?"

"I am going nowhere, like all of us on this earth. But at least I am back in Roma. *Grazie a Dio!* I can't stand to leave it. Roma is the only place with always something every day to kill the boredom."

Gianandrea took my shoulders in the grip of his strong two hands and gave me a friendly shake. Then he sat down at the table with me.

"Vincenzo! *Un' altro bicchière, per favóre,*" I called through the open restaurant door.

Vincenzo stuck his head out, recognized my guest, bowed and greeted him respectfully. *"Buòna séra, dottóre!"*

Italy still preserves the various titles of respect. I have been teaching English in Rome, teaching to finance my learning, but, with no Ph.D., I hardly consider myself a *professóre*, as Vincenzo always addresses me. Gianandrea, however, merits his honorific.

Gianandrea is a forensic pathologist, on the staff of the Santo Spirito Hospital and a professor at the University of Rome. There is no more renowned expert on disease and death in all Italy. Just a few weeks before, I had come across his name in *La Repùbblica* in connection with the investigation of the murder of a countess, supposedly by her enraged husband, who had caught her in adultery with a well-known male model.

Vincenzo brought out the glass I had requested and placed it on the table. I filled the glass with Frascati from the *litro fiasco* and passed it to Gianandrea.

"What *problèma culturale* of Roma are you brooding about today, eh?", Gianandrea asked me. *Omosessuali* in the court of Nero? *Òrgie* in Il Vaticano? The influence of syphilis on the decrees of the First Ecumenical Council?"

"Religion. I've been thinking about Rome and religion."

"What?! You will never come to the end of thinking about that. And thinking and drinking at the same time! No, Normano, that is not a good methodology. Do you think that I drink while I dissect the corpses? Certain things go together, certain things do not. Drink and dance and then make love, *cèrto*. But drink and think,—no.

"My poor Normano, you have not learned anything from Roma yet. I judge you, I sentence you, to ten more years, no, to a lifetime, in Roma. You know, '*Roma, non basta una vita*', how Signore Silvio Negro says; 'one lifetime not enough for Rome'."

"I want to understand something about religion. That was one of the reasons I came back to live in Rome."

"A bad reason, Normano. You should come to Roma to live and to enjoy. Religion,—there is no religion here. Superstition, *sì*, but religion, no. You want religion? Go to Israel and live in Gerusalémme."

Gianandrea took a deep swallow of the wine and looked across the table at me, that usual expression of sly deviltry on his face. He is a handsome man of Italianate type, a face like Apollo, but a middle-aged Apollo, the strands of gray well-established among the black waves of his hair.

"Religion, eh?", Gianandrea said. *"Bène*, OK, I will help you with your research, one *intellettuale* to another. In Torino, I just had a most interesting experience. Maybe it will tell you something about religion.

"What does all your thinking and brooding tell you about *relìquie*,—what's the word in English?"

"Relics."

"Sì, lo stèsso, relics. What do you know about them?"

"Rome has plenty, that's for sure. The pilgrims have always come to Rome for the relics, for some contact with the saintly heroes of their faith."

"Contact, ah, *sì*, contact, my dear Normano. Do you know that, when I was twenty years old, back in Milano, I loved a girl so much—I was *pazzo* about her, I worshipped her—, that I used to go a-round with a piece of her underclothes inside my shirt? Underclothes she had worn but not washed. I stole it from her, didn't tell her, kept it under my shirt. And, when I was away from her—*Dio*, my heart still pounds when I think of it!—, I used to take out the underclothes and place it against my face and think of her."

Gianandrea saw the startled look on my own face.

"Normano, are you shocked? Did you not do something like that some time? Did you not worship some girl?"

"I...I...", I stammered.

Gianandrea smiled in pleasure at his reminiscence, then continued: "Now for the religion. If I was a good Christian and I was in love with Sant'Agnese, I suppose I would steal her underclothes and go about with it under my shirt.

"Oh, what happened in Torino...But first, Normano, tell me what you know about the *reliquie*, the relics of Roma."

"Rome is the grand repository of Christian relics," I told Gianandrea. "First of all, of course, there are the bones of the catacombs, where hundreds of thousands of early Christians had themselves interred. Then, in the Middle Ages, all those nameless innocents were designated as saintly martyrs, and the catacombs were ransacked for their bones, because the bones of martyrs were powerful spiritual magic."

"What, no bones left in the *catacòmbe*?", Gianandrea asked.

"Just a few fragments remain in the niches, most of the bones snatched away by the traffickers in relics."

"A Christian has to make a living, even if from the dead," Gianandrea put in. "*Altrettanto*, who am I to judge? I make my own living from the dead, do I not? But I am not such a good Christian."

"It was martyrdom that gave the relic of the saint its powerful magic. Martyrdom was the assurance of eternal salvation."

"I kill myself! Now I live forever!", Gianandrea exclaimed.

"Yes, that's the way the early Christians thought. Suicidalists."

"Now only a *musulmano* thinks like that. Normano, do you ever ask yourself why most of the *santi* and *mártiri* were *vérgine?*"

"You're right, they were. Celibacy, chastity was a prime Christian value."

"A *vérgine* for life! Now I know why they all wanted to die." Gianandrea twitched, then shook himself, as if he was covered with ants.

"Yes, virgin-martyr was a winning combination. There are many tales in Christian lore about the tenacity of girls maintaining their virginity even unto death. One was Saint Agnes, whom you mentioned."

"What a waste! *Schifóso!*", Gianandrea exclaimed.

"Many of the relics of Rome are artifacts of the martyrdoms," I continued. "For example, there is the arrow that pierced the chest of Saint Sebastian, the grill that Saint Lawrence was roasted on, the chains that bound Peter, and other such paraphernalia of martyrdom."

"But what about the stronger magic?", Gianandrea asked. "The bodies, the bones, the physical *santi-vérgini* themselves?"

"Well, as you might know, the heads of Peter and Paul are in the canopy over the Lateran altar. The head of John the Baptist is in San Silvestro in Capite... Oh, and the rest of the body of Peter, or so they have claimed since Pius XII conducted the excavations, has always been under the altar of St. Peter's in the Vatican."

"But, Normano, the strongest Christian magic is not in San Sebastiano or San Lorenzo or San Silvestro or even San Pietro. What about the most powerful of all magic, that of *Il Grade Mártire, Gesu Cristo* himself?"

"Of course his relics arouse the most intense Christian devotion..."

"...would sell for the premium price, *sénza scónto.*"

"Certainly. Well, of his relics, we have in Santa Croce in Gerusalémme a piece from the cross, along with a nail used in the crucifixion, and the crown of thorns…"

"What more of *Gesu Cristo*?"

"Oh, any little thing mentioned in the gospels is likely to have turned up in some church or other."

"What about the strongest, most powerful of all magic, the body itself?", Gianandrea asked. There was malicious mischief in his face.

"In light of the doctrine of the Resurrection, your question, Gianandrea, is blasphemous."

"*Dio* forgive me. You too pardon me please, Normano, but your research on relics has not been thorough enough. There is magic, magic *poténte*, from the body of *Gesu Cristo* himself, right here in Roma."

"What do you mean?"

"Now I tell you something. Do you not know that, here in Roma, you can find some of the hair of *Gesu Cristo*? Some of his blood? And, to go with the blood—as a cocktail, *fórse*—how about some of the milk from the pure *vérgine* breast of *Santa Maria* herself?"

"What?!"

"*Sì, davvéro*. The sweet milk that nourished the *bambino*. From the pure, lovely breast of *Santa Maria* herself. Have you ever thought about those breasts? So lovely, so white...*Ma!* Maybe not so white, because she was *giudèa...*"

"Gianandrea, please!"

"Normano, I report only what the churches of Roma have as relics. The fault of respect is not mine. There are even more relics of the body of *Gesu Cristo...*"

"I'm afraid to find out."

"In San Salvatore della Scala Santa, they have the umbilicus of *Gesu Cristo*. Did your mother keep yours, Normano? Someday, if you become famous, it will be worth something. Another church in Roma has—I know you Protestant, you skeptic, won't believe it, but it is true—the product of the circumcision, the little foreskin itself."

"You're joking!"

"No, no joking when we talk religion. I report to you the truth. You don't read about it in the guidebooks, Il Vaticano does not advertise it, but it is there. I myself have read the documentation. What a treasure! What magic *potènte!*"

"It sounds pagan to me."

"*Pagano? Sì*, Roma has always been *pagana*. The Christians just changed the pagan sex-love of living bodies to the love of *vérgine* dead bodies. It is all *idolatrìa*."

"Well, Gianni, you certainly give me something to think about."

"Oh, I will give you a lot more to think about," Gianandrea promised. "Do you know about *La Santa Sindone*?"

"Something, yes."

"*La Santa Sindone*. What do you call it in English?"

"The Shroud of Turin."

"*Shrout? Shroud?* What a word in your English! I feel, when I try to say it, my face makes a funny expression."

"Well, it's not a word in everyone's vocabulary, and I suppose it's not very euphonious."

"But all people should know the word, because it is the relic of the magic most *pòtente* in all the world! What do you know about *La Santa Sindone*, the *shroud*, Normano?"

"Well, it is reputed to be the burial cloth of Jesus Christ. It is a long linen cloth, about twelve feet—four meters—, upon which the crucified body was supposedly laid. There is an imprint or stain or some kind of image on it, of the back of the body on one half and of the front of the body, including the face, on the other. It is as if the body was laid on the cloth, then the cloth was folded over the top of the body, and, somehow, the image of the whole body, front and back, is on the cloth...That's about as much as I know about it."

"But is it, is it really the burial cloth of *Gesu Cristo*?"

"How should I know? Most unlikely."

"More unlikely than the umbilicus?...than the foreskin of the circumcision? Unlikely, *sì*. Every *miràcolo* is unlikely. That is why it is *miràcolo*. Normano, you unbeliever, you skeptic!"

"Funny you should mention the Shroud of Turin. Just a week or so ago, I bought an image of the face of the Shroud. It is imprinted on cloth, a beautiful reproduction, although the face is really a painted enhancement..."

"Imprinted on cloth, you say? Just like the original! But why would you, a skeptic, want such a relic?"

"To me, it's not a relic. It's just a souvenir, *un ricòrdo da Roma.* And I find the medium, printed cloth, quite unusual. I've bought other artwork reproductions, some on cloth. You Italians make the finest art reproductions."

"*Cérto.* We make the art, we fake the art. What other art copies have you bought?"

"Oh, some of the standard images. You know, the *David* of Michelangelo, the *Primavera* of Botticelli..."

"Nude David, nude Venus, nude *Gesu Cristo*! Sometimes I worry over you, Normano...And *La Santa Sindone* itself,—do you consider it art...or relic?"

"Let's say, artifact. A cultural curiosity if ever there was one. Something pathological, definitely pathological."

"My specialty exactly!", Gianandrea exclaimed. "And now you are talking to the *maèstro*, not the religion expert, not the art expert, but the pathology expert."

"Oh, something else...," I said. "I had a Jesuit professor of theology who was a devotee of the Shroud of Turin. He even made a television program on it; they used to broadcast the program in Chicago every Good Friday. Anyway, he claimed that he could detect, upon the eyes of the man of the Shroud, coins inscribed with the name of Tiberius Caesar."

"Coins! *Mìo Dio!* For what? To pay Charone for the *passàggio* across the *Stige* River to the Underworld?"

"My own thought, exactly. Pagan again. Most unJewish."

"What *giudèo* would let a drachma go away and be gone with the dead?"

"It wasn't a drachma. It was a lepton," I informed Gianandrea.

"Drachma, lepton, *lire italiane*, U.S. dollar, what difference? To *Cesare* what to *Cesare*, to *Dio* what to *Dio*. No, *Gesu Cristo* took no money with him to Heaven."

"Most observers consider the coin a figment of the good Jesuit's excited imagination."

"*Figment-of-imagination?* That's what all relics are,—*figment*, I think the word means not real, am

I right?—of imagination. Yes, all love, even love of the dead, is imagination.

"Now, Normano, what I want to tell you about... When I was in Milano, I met by chance an old colleague of mine. He was involved in the investigation of *La Santa Sindone.* We talked and talked, and are such good friends, and you know how persuasive I am...*Quindi*, I went with him to Torino and saw *La Santa Sindone*, the famous Shroud of Turin, myself."

"You did?"

"Saw it and studied it most carefully. Now I know about *La Santa Sindone.* I, the pathologist, can explain it."

"But I thought they exhibited the Shroud only once or twice every century..."

"Correct, but this was the time, four hundred years since *La Sindone* arrived in Torino. Three million people came to Torino to see it. Three million *pellegrini*,—think of it! What else could get three million people to go to Torino, except *La Santa Sindone*?

"*Allóra.* At the end of the *esposizióne*, Umberto, who owns *La Santa Sindone*, Umberto, our King of Italy who never was king, gave permission for five days of scientific study of the *Sindone*."

"Come to think of it, I had heard there would be such a project."

"*Davvéro*, it was done. And I was there! You know, there were about thirty scientists, mostly

Americans. Americans,—skeptics like you! Even maybe an atheist touching *La Santa Sindone*! Why Americans? Because they have the technology. Imagine, Normano, they brought the technology they used to send a man to the moon, the NASA technology, to study *La Santa Sindone*! Two different worlds, two different minds, eh? Twentieth-century science against superstition *medievale*! American skeptics and *agnòstici*, atheists, skeptics, attacking a treasured relic of Italy. Oh, they permitted a few Italians to participate, like my colleague, but, how we all know, the world and all in it now belong to the Americans."

"Why did they permit the experiments? Do they want to authenticate the relic or debunk it?"

"*Debunk*?,—another funny word of your English. I suppose it means prove *La Sindone* is not *autèntica*. Oh please, Normano, don't be too simple! *La Chiesa Catòllica* does not approve *La Santa Sindone*. Why not? Because it has nothing to do with Roma. It is out of the control of Il Vaticano. Remember I said it belongs to Umberto, *un polìtico*. Il Vaticano probably wishes that *La Sindone* is proved *falso e finto* by a debunk, so that the three million *pellegrini* will bring their money here to *Roma*, maybe to see La Veronica instead."

(The Veronica is another cloth with the reputed image of Jesus, but of the face only. It resides in St. Peter's in the Vatican. It has not been exhibited in my lifetime, as far as I know. The Vatican is thus missing out on a lot of potential revenue, according to Gianandrea's reasoning.)

"*Dunque.* I was in the Palazzo Reale in Torino, where they did the experiments. I was there all the five days. I examined *La Santa Sindone* myself, unofficially, of course. I am too well-known a man for them to kick me out! They were happy to have another Italian around, to protect *La Santa Sindone* against the Americans.

"Don't think it was all pure science there. No. There are many who want to prove, who want to disprove,—*debunk*, that new word you just gave me. Why? Because of the magic *potènte. Anché*, the proof, or the disproof, of the story we read in the four *Vangeli*, the story of the death that leads to life eternal! Death, what I don't know about death!"

At this point Vincenzo brought out a menu for Gianandrea. I myself had already ordered a salad and the trout that I had inspected, approved, and selected, to be complemented by the white wine of Frascati.

Gianandrea waved away the menu. He knew what he wanted,—*rigatoni all'incarcerata*, the specialty of the house at Vincenzo's. A rich concoction of pasta, veal, and peas in a heavy cream sauce, *rigatoni all'incarcerata* is like Rome itself,— exquisite at first taste, whetting the appetite at the same time that it satisfies it, then so cloying that you know you will never be able to finish it. I myself can take *rigatoni all'incarcerata* only in a half-portion, but my friend is a man of immense animal appetites. Gianandrea always consumes the full portion.

The rest of our conversation continued through the serving and the eating of the courses of the meal. The wine flowed along in the current of Gianandrea's story:—

"*Béne*, there I was in Torino. I was curious about *La Santa Sindone*. I am a pathologist, am I not?

"After the *exposizióne* was finished and all the three million *pellegrini* paid their bills and went home, the American scientists had their chance to do their experiments. They were given only five days. Five days, why only five days? *La Santa Sindone* is lying around for two thousand years to serve religion, and they expect science to solve its problem in only five days?

"*Comùnque*, the Americans worked around the clock, to try to finish all their planned experiments in the five days. But you can't do science like that.

"What expensive equipments they brought in, the best American NASA technology! They made a special aluminum table for the laying-out of *La Santa Sindone*; the table revolved, so that the Americans could examine *La Sindone* from all the angles. And they had photographic equipments, and all other equipments,—I did not know what it all was.

"There were problems with the electricity. The Palazzo Reale is old, Torino is old, Italian technology is old. So, sometimes, *poh!*, the Americans were in the dark. *Una commèdia,* Normano!

"And watching all the time, the *monsignore.* He did not permit the Americans to cause any harm to *La Santa Sindone.* No cutting of *ricórdi,* no souvenirs, please! When you do an autopsy, you must cut into the body, you must do harm. Harm, what harm can you do to the dead, eh? But the *monsignore* did not permit the Americans to cut off even one *filo.*

"The Americans did experiments of chemistry and physics. I wanted to ask them what they were doing, but they were too busy to talk to me. They were always watching the clock, working fast day and night for the five days, now one group, now another without stopping. You Americans put all your *energìa* to send a man to the moon; we Italians still want to go to heaven! Religion is our technology for that.

"When one group left and another not yet arrived and set up, I was able to examine *La Santa Sindone* myself, but only by looking, looking with the eyes of a pathologist."

"What did you see?", I asked.

"All the injuries there, all the suffering, exactly to the words of the four *Vangeli!* What you only read as true, on *La Santa Sindone* you see as true. I see, I must believe! *Crocifissione,* most accurate, I think...But the blood, too red."

"What conclusions did the scientists come to?", I asked.

"*Boh!* I don't know. They only took the data. After the five days, they all went back to America, to the NASA laboratories to figure out the data, using more sophisticated equipments, I suppose. I think it will be years before they make any conclusions.

"But I already know the answer. The human eye, *my* eye, can see more than the NASA photographic equipments. The human brain, the experienced brain, like mine"—(and here Gianandrea pointed to his head and winked at me)—"can solve a problem quicker than any computer. I just walked into the *salóne*, and, when I looked at *La Santa Sindone* for the first time, I solved the problem immediately. *Presto!*"

Gianandrea snapped his fingers.

"You did? And what's the answer?"

"Wait, Normano. I have to tell you the story I want to tell. It is about *La Santa Sindone*, but it is more interesting than *La Santa Sindone*."

"What is it? Please tell me."

Gianandrea gave a little wave that meant "Be patient". He took some forkfuls of the *rigatoni all'incarcerata*, washed it down with the wine, then continued:

"*Dunque*...The *salóne* in the Palazzo Reale, where they were examining *La Santa Sindone*, was a very crowded place. All the equipments, all the scientists, technicians, the workers of the Palazzo, and the *monsignore*, and my colleague, and myself...And there were also two—how do you say it?—*religióse...*"

"You mean nuns?"

"*Sì.* An old one and a young one. They were there to work with—*cucire...*"

"They were sewing?"

"*Sì e no.* There was a cloth attached to *La Santa Sindone,* and the two nuns had to break the sewing to remove the attached cloth, and later, I think, they would sew the cloth back on. Women's work.

"You know, Normano,—I tell you this to help you with your research on religion—, there are two kinds of *religiósa* nun. The first kind is the *vérgine* who is not really a woman. I mean, she is a woman in her body, but not in her feelings. She hates men and the idea of sex. As a *religiósa* nun, she can escape both, and be honored besides. But there is the other kind of nun, a *vérgine* too, a woman who loves, but who wishes to love only in the most pure way. And so, she becomes a nun and loves only *Gesu Cristo. Fortunato* is *Gesu Cristo* to receive such love! *Sfortunato* are all the men who could receive that love, but do not, because of *Gesu Cristo*!

"The first nun, the old one, was, I think, of the first kind I said. But the second nun, the young one, was, I am sure, of the second kind, who loves with a strong love, but a pure love. No human man—not even I!—has ever received such strong love as the *vérgini* have given *Gesu Cristo*!

"As I said, I was very interested in the experiments on *La Sindone*. But the *salóne* was so crowded, and no one would answer my questions, that I was frustrated. I was going to leave and come back to Roma.

"But then I thought, 'Gianandrea, why do you always want to live in the land of the dead? Are not the living bodies more interesting than the dead ones?'

"So, I looked at the young nun most closely. She was *bèlla*, a face from a painting by Raffaello—or, as I know you like, Pompeo Batoni. Her body,—I didn't know. Who can guess what is under the clothes they wear, the clothes that conceal all?

"As the scientists worked, the eyes of the young nun were wide open, wide open, like this—"

And here Gianandrea pulled up his two hands and flared his fingers, while drawing back his lids into a fixed stare of fascination.

"She was looking hard—like this—at *La Santa Sindone*. Not a scientific interest, I don't think. *Anché*, she seemed *nervósa*, and afraid. When a scientist handled *La Sindone, fórse* too roughly for her, she would—*sussultare...*"

"*Sussultare?* Does that mean flinch or wince?"

"It means, do this..."

Gianandrea did, indeed, make a gesture like a wince.

"Anché, scomporsi..."

"Upset. She got upset. Was she afraid that the scientists would harm the Shroud?"

"Afraid, *sì*. But why afraid? It was not her job. It was the job of the *monsignore* to protect *La Santa Sindone*. There was nothing to be afraid of, for harm to *La Sindone*. The American scientists had no religion. It is only the religious people who do harm to sacred objects.

"As I watched the *vérgine*, I wanted to know her. So I went over and began to talk to her. *Sorèlla* Felicità was her name, a nun of the group of San Giuseppe.

"Oh, Normano, how I did love her voice! It was *dolce, un sussuro* such as a man likes to hear from a woman just before sex. My heart was pounding! But she took no notice of me, so hard did she look at *La Santa Sindone*. And I am not an old man or an ugly man! Why could she not look at me with that look that she gave to *Gesu Cristo?* If I was *Gesu Cristo*, how I would love to hear that *dolce* voice speaking to me in love, when she makes her prayers!

"It is not easy for a man such as myself, that loves women, that has loved many women, that many women have loved...It is not easy, when a *bèlla vérgine* pays to me no attention. Yes, I know she is *bèlla* and *vérgine* and young, but I am not old, I am still *bèllo*, I am *simpàtico*. What could I do? *Sorèlla* Felicità didn't care to speak to me, she didn't look at me. She only looked at *La Santa Sindone*. I am jealous of *Gesu Cristo!*

"As I said, there were five days of experiments, with no stops. But humans cannot work five days with no stops. So, the scientists worked in small groups, one group, then the next, all of them eating or pissing or sleeping when they could between the times of doing their experiments. *Pazza programma!*

"Do you think the *monsignore* stood all five days at the door watching? Or the old nun? No, they sent substitutes. But *sorèlla* Felicità, she did not leave the room, she did not leave *La Santa Sindone.*

"No, what I am speaking is not right. She left sometimes. Even a *vérgine* must eat and use the toilet and sleep. But I never was there when she was not. And I spent a lot of hours there...Not because of *La Sindone.* Because of *sorèlla* Felicità."

Gianandrea paused for more forkfuls of the *rigatoni,* two swallows of the wine, and then continued:

"Now I tell you more. When one group finished an experiment, before the next group came in to set up their equipments, *sorèlla* Felicità would come close to *La Santa Sindone.* And she would arrange it on the table, pull out a corner, make it flat where it was disturbed. She would touch only the edge of *La Santa Sindone,* most carefully, near the edge. Such a touch! If only I could receive such a touch on my naked skin! *Magari!* If only!

"*Sorèlla* Felicità would examine everything on *La Santa Sindone.* Not with the eyes of science.

With the eyes of love! Nobody, not the *monsignore*, not the old nun, thought anything about it. But I did. *Io!* I know the look on the face of a woman that loves, even if she is a *vérgine* that loves.

"I said about the problems with the electricity. On the third day of the experiments, all the lights went out in the *salóne*. Too much NASA technology drinking the old electricity of Italy. So, the scientists all left. Who can do science in the dark? I myself was outside the *salóne*, but close to the door. The *salóne* was all dark. No electricity, and it was night, and the windows were covered with black, so the scientists could do their photography.

"Then, in a sudden, the lights came back. I looked through the doorway and there I saw ...*sorèlla* Felicità, her fingers upon the skin of the naked man of *La Santa Sindone*! She was touching him in the dark! When the lights came back, she was shocked and looked up, right into my eyes! She pulled her hand back, then in a hurry went away from *La Santa Sindone*.

"And I saw on her face her thought. A thought that was a sin! A *vérgine* is a woman, Normano. *Gesu Cristo* was a man. A woman must love a man, as *Dio* Himself created."

"Was she embarrassed by your catching her doing that?"

"*Cèrto*, embarrassed. And guilty too. But why guilty? It is normal, is it not? Fortunately, the *monsignore* did not see, the old nun did not see. Only I saw.

"Then I went over to *sorèlla* Felicità and spoke to her pleasantly, so she would not be afraid that I would say anything to the *monsignore* or the old nun. And, Normano, it was exciting! It is exciting for a man to be near a woman who is excited, even if she is not excited for him...Do you think that strange, Normano? Do you think me a strange man?"

"It's a strange story you're telling me, that's for sure, Gianni. But I don't know what is strange and what is not. Some of what I have done seems strange to me now. How can I, then, find others strange?"

Gianandrea, seeing Vincenzo look out the door solicitously, held up the empty *litro fiasco* for a refill of Frascati.

"Think of it, Normano. *La Santa Sindone* has its *esposizióne* only one time or two times each hundred years. And even in the *esposizióne*, you cannot go close, you cannot touch. But the examination by the scientists,—that was *sorèlla* Felicità's chance, the only chance in her life, to be close, to touch, to feel the pure love for *Gesu Cristo* close to her!

"*Allóra*, on the fourth day, it seemed that *sorèlla* Felicità did not care if someone saw how she felt about *La Santa Sindone*. She paid no attention to anyone. It was as there were only two people in the *salóne*, a woman and a man, *sorèlla* Felicità and *Gesu Cristo*. *Che devozióne!*

"Another time, again as one group had left and the other not yet arrived with the equipments, I saw her touch the body of *La Santa Sindone*, not only the edge of the cloth this time or the outline of the *figura*, but the body, about where the heart is!

"Each day, *sorèlla* Felicità became closer to *Gesu Cristo*, in her mind, I mean. First she could only look, then only touch the edge, then from the edge toward the center, then to touch the heart itself, *cuor' di Cristo*! Did she want to bring that heart to life, that heart to pound, to pound with love of her?

"And when the scientists worked, she never took her eyes off *La Santa Sindone*. No, I change that. Sometimes what they did seemed to her— can I say?—painful; she had to close her eyes for a moment, as if the scientists were hurting the man she loved.

"You know, Normano, I do autopsies, because the family wants to know why the person died. But do you think that a lover can watch the autopsy of a loved one? They want to know, but they cannot bear to watch. Love hates science. *Sorèlla* Felicità hated the scientists and all that they were doing. She didn't say anything, but I knew, I observed that. Love hates science.

"The *monsignore*, the old nun, all the scientists,—none of them recognized the feelings of *sorèlla* Felicità for the man of *La Santa Sindone*. Only I did. Not because I am a doctor, a medical scientist. I saw, I understood, because I am a man that has loved women, that has had women love me, that knows what a woman in love looks like, even if she is a *vérgine religiósa.*"

Gianandrea paused in his story to scoop up more of the *rigatoni all'incarcerata,* which was at risk of becoming neglected and cold.

During the silence, I wondered whether my friend was interpreting *sorèlla* Felicità's behavior all wrong, was being carried along by his own overheated erotic imagination into an extended fantasy.

But then, the mound of pasta having been reduced to the bottom of the bowl, Gianandrea went on to dispel my doubts.

"*Buòno…Delizióso.*

"*Allóra…*It was the last day, the fifth day. And now the scientists were in a hurry to finish all the experiments. They were behind the schedule, because of the problems with the electricity and other problems with their equipments. They had the *programma,* and they wanted to do all the things on the *programma. Sciènza pazza!*

"And then, no more time, time gone! *Fuòri,* scientists! Time to put *La Santa Sindone* to the bed for fifty, a hundred years. The scientists too were tired, so tired. They took themselves to the bed, like walking dead men.

"When the *salóne* was empty, empty except for some equipments and *La Santa Sindone* on the table, I saw *sorèlla* Felicità walk over to *La Santa*

Sindone, bend over, and kiss it! She thought no one saw, but I saw.

"Then she came out and locked the door. The *monsignore*,—he gave her the key before, when he went to the bed.

"I was tired too, Normano, but I didn't want to leave. Not because of *La Santa Sindone*. As I said, I already solved the problem of *La Sindone*. No, I mean I didn't want to leave *sorèlla* Felicità. I wanted to talk to her, but she walked right past me. Her eyes did not see me at all.

"*Allóra*, on the next day, I thought I would go back to the *salóne* of the Palazzo Reale. The scientists were going to be taking out their equipments. Maybe I could talk to them at last, find out something. When will I ever have another opportunity to learn something from NASA, eh?

"And I thought, 'Maybe *sorèlla* Felicità will be there. I must talk to her.' "

"What did you want to talk to her about?"

"I didn't know. I had this strange feeling, Normano. I don't know, *fórse* love, *fórse* jealousy, but something strong I felt for *sorèlla* Felicità.

"I arrived at the Palazzo very early. I still had the permission to go in. And I met my colleague there, by chance. So the two of us walked to the *salóne*. The door was open, but only a small opening. The inside of the *salóne* dark. The removing of the equipments not yet started. The scientists still sleeping.

"We went in, and I looked at *La Santa Sindone*. Something was wrong about it, something strange! It seemed to be, not a flat *sindone*, but a solid form. A solid form! I was afraid, Normano!

"I went over and looked. A human form, a human body inside *La Santa Sindone*, that was now folded over the body. My heart, what shock! *Mio Dio*, you can't imagine what I thought! What *miràcolo* was this? *Gesu Cristo* returned?"

Gianandrea clutched at his heart, almost overturning his glass of wine.

"My colleague, too, he saw what I saw and was afraid. It was dark, as I said. So, he went over to one of the windows of the *salóne* and pulled back the black cover the scientists did put there for their photographic purposes. And the new light of the morning sun came in, like this—"

Gianandrea drew his arms down and to the side, his hands parallel, as if describing a wide ray of the entering sun.

"The sun came in...on the face of *sorèlla* Felicità! *Sorèlla* Felicità, sleeping with *Gesu Cristo* on *La Santa Sindone*! Her hand pulling La Santa Sindone over her like a cover on the bed. *Dio! Dio!*

"I called her name, '*sorèlla* Felicità! *Sorèlla!*' She did not answer or move.

"I pulled back *La Santa Sindone*, and..."

Here Gianandrea needed a full swallow of the Frascati to enable him to continue.

"*Nuda, completamente nuda!* Her body pure white, like marble. Or a body like a fruit never ripe, because it has never seen the sun. Her body, always covered, now uncovered for the first time.

"Then her hand fell over the edge of the table, just a little. Her white hand. And I took her hand. A cold hand, *Dio!*, a cold hand! I felt for her pulse. Not sleeping, Normano, not sleeping. Dead!"

And here Gianandrea began to get upset, but he controlled himself.

After a cough and a clearing of his throat and a wiping of his eyes, he continued:

"Normano, her face! A look I know. I myself have put that look upon the face of some women. *Èstasi!*"

"Ecstasy!", I exclaimed, although Gianandrea needed no translation help in telling me what he wanted to express.

"*Èstasi!*", he repeated. . .

Gianandrea and I then fell into a long silence, as another Roman night descended around us. Our plates were now scraped clean, our glasses emptied.

At last, Gianandrea said, in a matter-of-fact voice, "My colleague did the autopsy. I talked to him on the telephone just this afternoon. Heart defect, from the birth, probably never diagnosed. We don't say someone died from *a broken heart.* That is romantic poetry, not medicine. Heart defect, a defect of the heart. Too much excitement, then a heart attack.

"Nobody knows this that I tell you, what happened. Nobody except my colleague and I and the old nun.

"*Comùnque*, we shut the door of the *salóne* and kept the scientists out. Love hates science! We placed the Sindone flat, as it was supposed to be. Then we took out the body of the *vérgine* in secret, in my car, back to the *convénto di religióse*. The old nun and my colleague and I put clothes on the body of *sorèlla* Felicità and placed her in her own small, narrow bed, where another nun found her later.

"*Giusto*, no *scàndalo*. What we did was not right, but there was no crime, was there? *De mortuis nil nisi bonum*, we say in *la lingua latina*. I could not bear to read the name of *sorèlla* Felicità in the newspapers, with such sensational things to be said about her. No. I think no one in Torino will discover our little *cospirazióne*.

"And you, *il mio amico* Normano, you will tell no one. Oh, in many years, after I am dead. What do I care then?"

After some minutes of my mulling over Gianandrea's story, I said to him, "I find something deeply disturbing in what you have told me."

"Disturbing? That is because you think and judge. Do not think and judge. Understand, accept! That is the lesson that Roma should teach you."

Looking at his watch and leaping to his feet, Gianandrea exclaimed, *"Mio Dio!* I am going to meet a *bèlla signorina*, a new nurse at Santo Spirito. How long it took for me to get her to accept! I have my reputation, you know. And my profession, which is not a romantic one to a *bèlla signorina*. And now I am late!"

Gianandrea threw some money on the table, said *"Buòna séra, professóre!"*, gave me a grand wave, and hurried off.

"Wait, Gianandrea!", I shouted after him. *"La Santa Sindone!* You said you solved the mystery of *La Santa Sindone*. Is it real, then, or fake?"

"Falso e finto," Gianandrea called, continuing his brisk pace down Via Castelfidardo.

"How do you know it's a fake?", I persisted, getting up from my chair, with half a mind to chase Gianandrea down the street to get the answer.

Gianandrea stopped, turned around toward me, and called out, *"Non è Gesu Cristo!* The man of *La Santa Sindone*...he is not circumcised!"

And, with that, Gianandrea disappeared into the murk of a Roman night.

Flippancies

246

Sex began in sin, they say. Sin began in sex, they say.

Even from my otherwise panerotic perspective, I have never been able to perceive how the Fall of Man as narrated in Genesis could be interpreted as a sexual sin. Any erotic exegesis of "The Tale of the Tree and the Trespassers" seems too fanciful and prurient to my critical sense. Horticultural symbolism does evoke sexual associations, but I think the old Hebrews had something else in mind when they told that sour story. I just cannot follow the alleged causality from an ambrosial picnic snack to the *pudeur* of being "naked and a-shamed". The forbidden fruit was not fornication.

Nonetheless, there are still those who interpret the Original Sin as a sexual transgression. They disregard the apple and assert instead that things really started to go wrong for mankind when Eve got her hand on the banana...Adam's!

247

Well, the question of human origins is a necessarily contentious one, affecting as it does our self-estimate as a species. We just can't let biological bygones be bygones. And we have to look at ourselves in the mirror every day.

In the ideological warfare between science and religious myth, the Darwinian scriptures rebut the

Jewish ones. When I read *On the Origin of Species* in my hammock on a tropical veranda, however, I found nothing offensive to myself in the critical scrutiny of plants, insects, and birds. T.H. Huxley was the troublemaker; he brought apes into the discussion.

And now we have to put up with Desmond Morris, who tells us confidently—never mind the significance of *the opposable thumb*—that the evolution from monkey to man was fully accomplished when the male tail moved around to the front.

248

The essential difference between Nature and culture was revealed to me, or, better, dropped from on high, when a pigeon in St. Mark's Square in Venice soiled my shoulder with its messy excrement.

Even before I got off the train, I had had the thought that no stay in Venice would be complete without that little incident. I had entered the city as a fatalist. My prophetic apprehension was duly vindicated.

Back in North America, I often used to stroll through rural fields and woods teeming with birds. They chirped and sang in the treetops above me, soared over my head catching insects, or flushed from the ground at my approach. I have stood under long Vs of migrating geese and flocks of ducks that wheeled in the air and dropped into a pond with a great splash and clatter. I have seen an entire grove rustling with cheeping armies of sparrows and chickadees. And I have approached huge oaks and cottonwoods blackened and burdened by a raucous horde of starlings, crows, grackles, and blackbirds. Yet, in the midst of all such avian abundance in Nature, I don't recall ever once having been dumped upon. The birds and I seemed to keep our respective, respectful distances.

But after just five minutes in St. Mark's Square,—shit on my shoulder. The pigeon may once have been another of God's creative ideas, but when it joined the urban masses, it was metamorphosed into an aerial manure spreader.

I see the main achievement of culture as an increment of excrement. The forests are full of animals, but I would have to walk long and far to find evidence of them on the bottoms of my shoes. There is, of course, scat, but it is scattered. In Venice, however, every dog uses humans to spread upon the sidewalk the message of its coprophilic calling card. While looking up to avoid the blitzkrieg of the pigeons, I step onto a dung land mine laid by the canines.

And that, the moral to my anecdote, dear readers,—don't be squeamish—, is what urban culture is all about: Shit from above, shit below. Sly and circumspect must be our course through a city, if we hope to stay pure.

The contemporary ecology movement may be considered a reactionary fastidiousness, an attempt to keep our noses up and out of the mounting piles. Such reformism is laudable, albeit futile. Nature just cannot process so much stinking excremental avalanche and transform it into a fecund compost. Nor will a lily spring up from the mountainous inert excreta of modern technology; there will be no verdure out of such ordure.

The waste disposal processes of Nature are overworked. The ecological state of the world is like a clogged, choked-up, overflowing toilet, to which we insist on adding more contents. Our fate, then, looms before us: A mass smotheration in the privy of progress.

Now, these are certainly unpleasant images and metaphors. Yet, anyone who honestly chronicles our time finds himself becoming more and more articulate in the phraseology of scatology.

The fouling crap of a typical pigeon of St. Mark's Square provides a parable on culture.

. . . Yes, I washed it off my shoulder, but I needn't tell you what I stepped upon on my way to the fountain.

249

It is not only the manure of crowded animals that fouls our cultured lives. Civilization creates an environment in which we humans excrete upon ourselves and upon one another. I refer not to alimentary wastes, but to the offal and flatus of our combustive technology.

How much better is one's own sweat and grime from hard labor or even the smell of a lathered horse than this noxious, choking, flatus billowing out from our vehicles. No one wanted to walk and carry, so we invented automobiles and buses and trucks and trains. Now we ride, but we cannot breathe.

Rome is fumigated by the wafted gases from the bowels of internal combustion engines. Today's Romans, having only diesel smoke and fumes and soot to breathe, gasp in the stifling atmosphere of technology's outhouse.

Machines fart in our faces, and we tolerate it, whereas our farming forefathers always kept their distance well behind the horse. This is progress? This is modern enlightenment?

250

In a gospel episode, we read about the changing of water into wine; and it was considered a one-time miracle.

Every day millions of Italians change wine into water; that is the continuing miracle of the Mediterranean metabolism.

If only the Magician were here to collaborate with the Italian kidneys. Then water-wine-water-wine transformations could be carried on in a perpetual process, the end product of consumption miraculously transubstantiated back into the initial alcoholic reagent.

Imagine. Italy could dispense with the grape.

251

The spirit of Horace groans in anguish these days. All of us Epicureans are dismayed by a scandal that has just broken out. Some wines of Frascati and our Alban Hills have been found to be adulterated. Police raids have been made on the unscrupulous vintners' establishments, where the *fiasco* was being treated like a test tube and even harmful chemical concoctions were being labeled *vino*.

This situation is an affront to both health and culture. If anything could rouse the usually pacific Italians to the frenzy of a lynch mob, it would be the willful contamination of the peninsular *aqua vitae*. Has our modern world come to such a pass that one cannot even look into the clear, wholesome simplicity of a glass of white wine without apprehension?

The proprietor of a *rosticcerìa* near Trevi where I often have lunch (always accompanied by some *vino bianco*) joked about the scandal in an attempt to mollify and reassure his concerned customers. I myself do not take the prospect of being poisoned by my Mediterranean tonic so lightly. Oh Italy, what a disgrace! It's almost enough to make one pack up and move to France.

252

Upon my first visit to the Vatican Museums, I was annoyed to see that all the classical sculptures of male nudes had had their genitals plastered up and frosted with a discreet leaf. Instead of maleness jutting forth in proud prominence, the cynosure of the body was a piece of autumnal rubbish.

If an ancient Greek or Roman could have seen such a monster as a man whose crotch sprouted vegetation, he would have run forthwith to Hesiod or Ovid with a tale to be included in their works, prefacing the report with "*Mirabile dictu!*".

The pagan mind itself was naked, fully eroticized, and free of the fig leaf of guilt, which was the crop of Christianity. The Vatican seems a bit ridiculous in its curious scruple, for, where the Greek merely depicted what Nature had provided, the Church hides under a cover of shame the creative scepter that God Himself gave to man.

The ancient pagan was innocent in his acceptance of our animality. Not so the Church, which retreated back to the supposed sexlessness of the vegetative world. Yet, it is not the leaf that is the generative organ, but, rather, the stamen, which is a sort of penis. The Vatican is as guilty of bad botany as of prudishness.

More significant than any whimsied mockery of eccentric shame and fig leaves is the fact that the Roman Catholic Church did preserve much of the heritage of antiquity from destruction by righteous iconoclast vandals. That may have been due to a persistence of pagan Roman aesthetics in the Christian Italian. The characteristic vitality of the pagan could not be fully extinguished by the gloomy life-denial of Christianity, at least among the vivacious Italian people (although other European southerners, the Spanish and Portuguese, did succumb to morbid otherworldliness).

The Vatican put crosses on the roofs of pagan temples and pubic foliage on nude male statuary, thus rendering both pagan architecture and sculpture morally acceptable. That happy stratagem preserved some of the magnificence of the classical world mostly intact beneath the seal of ecclesiastical approval. It is fortunate that Calvinism never took hold here in Italy, because it would have obliterated and extirpated every trace of the pagan classical.

The Italian mind has generally been a poor field in which to sow iconoclasm. That field is already fertile in its own Mediterranean produce,— *oleavitisficus*, that is, olives for health, grapes for wine and life-intoxication, and fig leaves for redeemed art.

253

Wandering past the storefronts on Via Condotti, I was reminded that Italy is a prolific producer of neckties, those loose nooses that modern men wear to no purpose.

A necktie, considered from the viewpoint of the economics of clothing, is merely an article of sartorial *conspicuous display*. However, the psychological symbolism of the necktie is intriguing and meaningful, haven't you told us, oh psychoanalysts?

An old acquaintance of mine, nicknamed Peaches because of his complexion, I suppose, is a salesman and a very dapper dresser. He told me this anecdote: Admiring one of his flashy neckties, a young girl he knew remarked, "That's a very sexy tie you have on, Peaches." To which he claims to have replied, "If you think that's sexy, you should see what it's pointing to."

In that snappy story, the symbolism of the necktie and the reason for wearing one are made manifest, to naïve girls as to psychoanalytic initiates. It is not socially acceptable for a man to exhibit his penis to the world to be admired, so he selects a flashy pointer and sartorial substitute. "You should see what I am pointing to!", the necktie proclaims.

I myself have always had a distaste for neckties. I have resolved never to spend a dollar on one, if I can make do with others' castoffs, when I need a tie for a formal occasion.

I share the strict utilitarian values outlined by Thoreau in "Economy", that is, clothing enough for warmth and comfort, and not a stitch or frill more.

Now, that is not to say that I do not possess some of that vanity toward that part of me that a necktie symbolizes. It is just that my thrift in this instance takes practical precedence over any cock's impulse to put on the silken plumage of ostentatious courtship.

A thoroughgoing naturalist, I prefer a plain open shirt. And dropped pants for the mating dance.

254

When a girl or woman has to stand in one place for a long time, she usually clasps her hands together in front. A boy or man in the same situation generally joins his hands together behind him, puts his hands in his pants pockets, or leaves his hands by his sides.

I interpret such poses as unconscious demonstrations of feminine modesty and male exhibitionism. She hides hers, while he displays his. She protects shyly, slyly, while he projects vainly. What could be more natural?

Clothes may conceal our parts, but our genital psychology stands naked.

255

Some women wear short skirts and are continually tugging and pulling them down to maintain a modicum of modesty. Other women wear long skirts, only to have to resort to discreetly raising them a little for attention.

That seems a perennial problem of the which-way-of-wiles.

There is an interplay, sometimes consonant, sometimes dissonant, between the psychology of the individual woman and the apparel that current fashion outfits her with.

The history of women's fashion is simply the many indecisive alterations in the strategy of attraction.

256

A woman's body is her burden...and her opportunity.

257

Continuing his role as critic of sculpture, Nathaniel Hawthorne described the Capitoline Venus as "a heavy, clumsy, unintellectual, and commonplace figure".

That seems to me a too-severe criticism of the statuesque goddess. *Heavy*? Well, she is solid marble. *Clumsy*? How can she be clumsy? She doesn't even move. *Unintellectual*? A goddess, un-like a mortal woman, is just as attractive with her head missing, as we see in plenty of museum examples. And *commonplace*? Those New England Puritan dames must have been more voluptuous than the stereotype has led us to believe.

A related aesthetic criticism occurred to me when, while gazing at the Capitoline Venus my-self, my mind wandered to the memory of some female nudes of Peter Paul Rubens:—When, at exactly what point of increase, does flesh become fat?

258

This morning in the Roman Forum, I stood upon the small ancient mound that is marked *Umbilicus Urbis Romae*. Imagine the significance of the site. As Rome itself is the Cosmopolis, the world-city, so, then, the *Umbilicus Urbis Romae* is nothing less than the *Umbilicus Mundi,* the navel of the world.

The symbolism of the human body, especially in sculpture, has been much on my mind lately. Inspired by this umbilical monument, let me indulge in a little whimsical anatomical geography. How about allocating the main parts of the body to various cities of the world? Corporal idolatry would be internationalized, and each chosen city would acquire an anatomical totem, a cult shrine to attract pilgrims and devotees.

I would place the monument, *Skull,* for example, in Johannesburg, on the continent where the many paleontological discoveries have so disturbed our conceptions of our human origins. Athens would lay claim to *Brain,* homage to the patrimony of the Greek philosophers. London would be a suitable location for the totem temple to *Hair,* out of deference to the famous portraits of that city's rulers and jurists.

The *Oculus Mundi* would be enshrined in Florence, because, during the Renaissance there, mankind opened its eyes the widest. Vienna would be the appropriate custodian of the world *Ear,* on the merits of her classical music heritage. I think I'll award the universal *Mouth* to Khajaraho in India, paying homage to Vatsayana's verbal oralism in certain instructive passages of the *Kama-Sutra,* and also remembering the eternal Indian hunger. *Nose* would be situated in Bergerac, no mere crude allusion to the typical townsfolk there.

Having finished the head, let's work down-ward:—

The sacrificial altar to *Throat* we erect as an-other of the many monuments of Vatican City, because the Church has succeeded in swallowing so much of human wealth and effort.

Shoulders would be deservedly located in Beijing, symbolizing the millennia of burdensome toil borne by the Chinese people. *Back* belongs to another Asian city, Tokyo, which so brilliantly adopted both Western technology and political du-plicity that much of the rest of the world has since viewed that city from behind.

My Rome is ever *Breast*, in topographical allu-sion to the breast-setting of its Seven Hills, in architectural allusion to the domes of its city-scape, and in cultural allusion to its traditional matriolatry. I would nominate Concord, Massa-chusetts as the town most deserving the guard-ianship of *Chest*, because Concord engendered some of the finest examples of manhood the Americans have thus far produced.

Arms reaching out from New York City repre-sent the accepting embrace of millions of immi-grants seeking a freer and better life. (All right, maybe that's not true anymore, but stereotypes are persistent symbols.) *Hand*, clenched in a fist, will find monumentalization in Berlin, character-izing Prussian militarism.

Rome is, as we have discovered, *Navel*, but *Belly* in its broadest sense should go to the *gemülichkeit* beer capital, Munich. *Buttocks* is Detroit.

Cities representative of the visceral organs are as follows:—

Heart has already found its home in Hollywood, the cinematic romance factory. *Lungs* might belong to any of several cities of Switzerland, where the pure Alpine air of democracy has long invigorated the breathing of human hope. Cairo is the most *Intestinal* city, digesting as it has such a large consumption of human history. Venice, ever fluid and flowing, is the city of *Bladder*. Calcutta,—the *Rectum* of the world.

Rome earns its third distinction—(I hope I'm not being too much of a local patriot here)—as *Womb*, but to Paris must go, mostly on the strength of Henry Miller's testimony, but also to give the French chauvins some satisfaction, the honor of being the pre-eminent community of *Genitals*.

Completing our corporal inventory and awards to cities most representative of human anatomy, we may erect the twinned-column monument, *Legs*, in Denver, ski-land. Finally, the site for *Feet* would be Jerusalem, in reminiscence of the destination of the forty years' heroic trek of the footsore through the desert dust. . .

Left for allocation is one more human part, that is, the *Soul*. You don't belong on earth, *Soul*. All souls go to Heaven. Be off with you!

And what about *Consciousness*? I'll put that into section 259, of course.

259

There is a salon in the papal apartment of the Castel Sant'Angelo that contains two salacious paintings of rural bacchanals, one by Poussin, the other by Dossi. Now what, I wondered, could such scenes of drunkenness and debauchery arouse in the minds of the celibate, august pontiffs?

Here a swooning satyr, there a fair maiden dozing off in intoxication, oblivious to the fact that her skirts are being lifted with lewd intent by a young rogue, all throughout tasty white breasts, bare or being bared, in the one work a male hand in a female lap, in the other a female hand on a naked male thigh, in both enough wine for a hundred Masses. . .Stop! Call in the censors! Are the Dominicans and Jesuits all asleep?

There was no papal prudery in the Renaissance Vatican. Even the most fervid anti-Catholic must find something appealing in the venereal rascality of Pope Alexander VI, for example. The fifteenth- and sixteenth-century popes made voluptuousness virtuous and ensconced themselves in surroundings of sumptuous sensuality. Their vice was carnal in source and classical in inspiration.

When the popes began to patronize the revival of ancient culture, they necessarily encountered naked mischief in the amorous art characteristic of the pagans. What could be done by the upholders of Christian values about the abundant classical celebrations of venery and the pleasures of the palate? If sensuality were eradicated from classical culture, what would remain?

— —(I saw in a bookstall in Piazza Esedra a Latin edition of Ovid, fully expurgated and Christianized for the refined reader by some priest, who must have done his editorial work with a pair of scissors. I would guess that more of Ovid went into the censor's wastebasket than into the proffered volume. The priest added bulk to his scrapbook of snippets by providing lengthy philological footnotes. If the censors had totally prevailed, the essential Ovid, like the essential classical culture, would now be in oblivion.)— —

Fortunately for us, the Renaissance popes were Italians true to their pre-Christian heritage. They did not decree amputation of every heroic phallus that emerged in erection out of the rubble of the Greco-Roman past. Those clerical reincarnations of certain old emperors were opportunistic aesthetes who baptized pagan culture. All beauty, even naked beauty, was from God, they argued with theological authoritativeness, and therefore beauty must be good. The pontiffs gave *ex cathedra* approval to art, even of the type that portrayed a happy immorality.

That vulgarian heretic, Martin Luther had to stand aside and view (to his spiritual chagrin, no doubt) the beatification of Petronius, Ovid, and Catullus.

The bacchanal was as culturally significant a liturgy to those popes as was Holy Mass. The

Counter-Reformation brought a reaction, true, but that was sour grapes in the Communion wine.

A complete concordance between the classical aesthetic and the world view of Christianity was impossible, of course. No dexterous synthesizer like Aquinas could succeed in that task, the Humanists of the time going through the motions but failing to convince the pious. Venus just would not robe up as the Blessed Virgin, nor would Bacchus take to the diet of locusts and wild honey espoused by John the Baptist.

Nonetheless, the Italians, with the connivance of the papacy, broke the monopoly of ascetic Christian values on culture and introduced a vital counterculture, the revived classical, out of which there gradually emerged another culture, our modern secular one.

The pall of the Christian death-cult that spread gloom over Europe for a thousand years was cast aside by the resurgent vitality of pagan *eros*. And it was the keepers-of-the-keys to the Kingdom of Heaven who were the principal perpetrators of that fortunate treachery. Alexander VI may well have said to a minister one day, "Cancel my saying of the Requiem; I have a bacchanal I want to attend instead."

The lives of those popes are, understandably, rued by ecclesiastical historians. The Renaissance popes and prelates lived too well, thus forsaking the orthodox Christian asceticism. Yet, lovers of humane values owe a homage of gratitude to those Christian priests, patrons who revived pagan art and culture, and who in their own lives demonstrated how the soul-sick should undertake their own rehabilitation by resuscitating the natural human being. Praise those popes and enjoy the pleasures!

260

Who would think that Thoreau's question, "Why should we live with such hurry and waste of life?", would be relevant to the Italians? The Romans scurry about as busy and industrious as Prussians, Dutchmen, or Luxembourgers. Rome seems to throb under the pressure of a constant rush hour. Crowds and cars and compulsion:— Work, work, work!

Here in a Mediterranean society? Whatever happened to *la dolce vita* and *dolce far niente*? (The two mottoes combined: *The sweet life, doing nothing.*) The native genius for living of the Italian race has been extinguished. Oh, curse of progress!

Nero and ye other refined voluptuaries, toss restlessly in your tombs as you witness the grand tradition of *otium* (leisure) and debauchery utterly abandoned in our twentieth-century Rome. A contemporary Roman might orgy, but only if he can schedule it sometime outside the work-week.

261

The Englishman wants a woman for companionship. The Frenchman wants a woman for romance. The Italian wants a woman for a bedmate and sparring partner. The American wants a woman for a trophy and domestic appliance.

262

Italian women are very assertive physically. They enjoy bumping their bodies aggressively against their men, and, when angered, carry on the argument in a corporal manner verging upon assault. The Italian woman is indeed a formidable animal.

Yet, despite the playful threat to life-and-limb that she poses to her man, the Italian woman is not dominating or castrating. She neither confronts nor undermines the man's self-estimate of virility and masculinity. The Italian woman is a lioness, strong but with a subdued ferocity. Somehow the lion feels himself stronger through her companionate strength.

American women I have known are self-contained and genteel, bland and deceitfully dependent. They want their men to feel strong mainly by contrasting themselves with their *help-less* consorts.

But the American woman is calculating. She uses the frigid silence of her detachment to emasculate the man. I have observed these *helpless* dominants leading around their de-sanguinated spouses cowering and tethered on a leash.

The totem-animal of the American woman is the bat, fragile and flighty, but a vampire draining the blood of masculinity from a victimized man.

I myself would risk a mauling for love, but when I detect the tiny sharp teeth behind the smile I grab my manhood and run.

263

In thinking of sex, the Englishman tut-tuts, the Frenchman winks, the Italian smacks his lips, the American rubs his palms together.

264

"Excuse me, but may I ask you a personal question?", she inquired.

I tensed defensively and put my guard up. What private *inner sanctum* of my soul did she intend to penetrate with her *personal question?*, I wondered.

It is a cautionary courtesy, that *excuse me* with which we prelude a personal question. She had warned me, so, while giving her permission to probe, I was wary. If the question was too personal, how could I politely communicate a definite NO TRESPASSING message? Young lady, aren't you being a bit presumptuous and intrusive and intimate to ask me a personal question after an acquaintance of only ten minutes?

Asking a personal question may be an erotic initiative. How soon you wanted to get into my clothes, under my skin, with your inquiry! The anomaly of genteel culture is that, before groping me, you apologize, "Excuse me, but may I please grope you?". A personal question is a verbal grope.

She glossed her forwardness with civility, while I tried to conceal my skittishness with agreeable acquiescence. "How close can I get to him?", I thought she must be asking herself. "How deep does she want to get in?", I asked myself.

An electric tenseness between us, I assented and awaited her personal question, all ready to conceal my private parts if her prying got too immodest.

The may-I-please and the yes-you-may thus dispensed with, she asked her personal question outright:

"How much money do you make on this job?"

What? *"How much money?"* I was bewildered, having covered all my pudenda to no purpose. I expected a personal question, but she asked me about money. Taken aback, I answered awkwardly, relaxing my self-defensive posture.

I had thought that she was going to get physical; instead, she got fiscal. What does money, an *it*, have to do with my person, me? *Personal* means my mind, soul, heart, and body. She asked about dollars and called it *personal.* What quirk of diction was that?

Money is no part of my naked person. Wary of being seduced into an intimate revelation, I was tricked into a topic of profanity. The hussy was an accountant in disguise.

...But pause. Let's examine this misunderstanding. Isn't she an American? When she asked her personal question, wasn't she saying something about the American values system?

In the United States, people will go into unashamed explicit detail about their bodies and their uses and abuses of others' bodies. They slit themselves open and spill their guts onto the marketplace. *Free speech.* Let's have it all out! That's called honesty, American honesty. The people have a right to know, ought to know. Anyone who would like to keep himself to himself is suspect; mustn't be antisocial with a rude "None of your business". Nothing is private in America; that would be unwholesome. There are no taboos, all must be told, nothing may be hidden...well, except for details about money. Money is the last private, sacrosanct American topic. An inquiry about money is a *personal question.* Ask an American his vices, but don't dare ask his salary or rent.

In America, the person is quantified. One's worth is calculated in an arithmetical manner. How much one has = how much one is. Net worth constitutes human value.

And, "If you're so smart, how come you're not rich?":—Another question I once had put to me by an American.

Upon such ludicrous values—promiscuous self-exposure and quantified quality—the Americans construct their values system. No wonder their love is a balance-of-payments. *Spiritual bankruptcy* must be an American term; there could be no better self-characterization. What is there left of the American person to question? When an American gets personal, after all, he or she is only talking about money. Money is, apparently, the *arcanum,* the *sancta sanctorum* of the American soul.

Do the Americans blush when they expose their money, as if their privates had popped out in public? Come to think of it, the inner wallet is concealed with a reserve not accorded the inner person.

When that young lady asked me her *personal question,* she wanted none of my person; she was just soliciting a sum. To her, the dollar is a personal attribute. If I had answered her question in an exact amount, would it have been obscene, a perverse self-exposure?

An American man's intimate incursion upon an American woman fills her till not with hot teeming seed but with an icy ejaculation of tinkling pennies.

265

I have had other absurd encounters.

When I was twenty years old, in Naples for the first time, a young man in the street offered me his sister for my enjoyment. My moral outrage was heightened, when, he pulling me by the arm through a doorway, I perceived, even in the deceptive dark, that what he was offering me for rent was not his sister, but his mother.

[186]

When the Soviet Union was opened to tourism, shortly after Khrushchev had pried the bolted door of Stalin's closed fortress, I found myself in a hotel corridor with a thin, pasty-faced girl of Leningrad. She took me by the hand, opened the door to a dark bathroom, seated me fully clothed on a toilet, closed and locked the door, sat herself astride me, and poured out upon me all her repressed ardor, but giving me the impression that what she was finding her thrill in was not passion, but treason.

In Maceió, Alagoas, Brazil one hot summer afternoon, I was bathing in a barrel in a secluded alley. A young woman, on her way to the public fountain for water, but apparently become misdirected among the byways, came upon me, looked at me, threw her clay pot aside, stripped off all her clothes, and jumped into the barrel with me, half the water and all of my dirt brimming over onto the ground.

In Recife, Pernambuco, Brazil, I happened upon a despondent young woman with one leg over a railing, on the brink of plunging herself several floors to the hard end to her life. I pulled her back from the brink and embraced her. Later, in her heartfelt gratitude, she brought both of us back to life.

In Brazil, too, an Amazonian Indian girl first remarked to me offhandedly, then proved most pointedly, a primitive fact of instinct that at once rendered the entire psychoanalytic theory of sex such cockeyed nonsense that I can no longer even think about it without bursting out laughing.

As I was just arrived in San Francisco, a woman in front of my hotel took one look at me, then threw herself at me as if I were the only man of gender normality in the entire city.

When I walked out of the Greyhound bus station in New York, a prostitute offered to give me that very night what I had been searching an entire lifetime for,—happiness!

And I recently enjoyed the bed of a famous pop singer, only to discover, from the menagerie of stuffed animals heaped upon the pillows, that she whose singing was so expressive of female passion was herself not a woman, but a little girl still.

266

Friendship lacks passion and intensity, so bored friends may be tempted to seek sex from each other. After all, a friend, like sexual drive, is always there. Why not, then, love her a little lower...But lust will lose the friend.

Sex lacks the constancy and continuity of friendship, so overenthusiastic lovers will often attempt to form a friendship with each other. The joy of friendship, they think, is an extension of the pleasures of intimacy. Why not, then, love her a little higher...But sublimation will extinguish animal sex.

You can see from my parallel paragraphs that self-seeking drive and empathetic companionability, sex and friendship, are incompatible. Sex parts friends. Friendship estranges lovers.

So, friends, do not touch each other. Lovers, do not get too chummy or confide in each other. If you muddle the carnal and the spiritual, you'll muddy both.

Friendship between men and women, if not impossible (as my mentor Nietzsche insists), does raise mutual suspicions and tensions, and so proves unwholesome. Same-gender sex is (despite Greek enthusiasms, ancient and modern) a rude bump against the sphincter of Nature or else a rub the wrong way. Therefore, I say to you, with the confidence of support from both philosophy and Nature:—Same-gender friends, other-gender lovers,—two absolutely distinct categories.

Hello, lady friend. I like you, but hands off!

Hello, lover. I love you, but let's not get personal about it.

267

She sits there on the chair, leaning forward over the table, rapt in empty admiration for the Hollywood Adonis who gazes at her and utters his inane, but oh-so-masculine sentences.

She smiles, all shy, all calculatedly coy, but needing. Brushing her hair back from her cheeks, she tilts one side of her face, then the other, toward him in that grimace smile young women make when trying to please.

He puffs up his chest and rattles on, all self-confident, seeking to impress, but already sensing that he has made his impression.

Pose faces pose across the table in a comic little pantomime. Teasing twit and obtuse stud, they face each other. Ah, the feints and moves and parries! Ah, the game!

268

Men are always plotting against women. For a base reason,—sex. Women are always plotting against men. For a noble reason,—marriage.

Men want bedmates, women want life-mates:— That is the dilemma involved in the traditional relations between the sexes. Still, the convergence of the divergences is that it is all plotting. Albeit their objectives are different, male leers and female looks-of-longing express the same desirous scheming.

My advice to women about how to deal with a man (no matter how pure and sincere he seems) is, "Always protect yourselves". Such counsel, however, may be unnecessary, because women seem to have an innate self-protective instinct. They deftly foil his plot, as they advance the cause of their own.

Men are such simpleton schemers, after all, pitifully inept in skirmishing against female wiles. Thou hot and cocky spider, beware the wasp entrapped in your web! She is shrewder and may sting deeper than you expect.

Oh what a subtle, self-laid trap we weave
When first we practice to deceive.

No man has ever yet, in the entire history of the human race, won a battle-of-wits with a woman. Therefore, I now extend to men my wise aforementioned advice: "Men, always protect yourselves!"

269

A misunderstanding between the sexes:—A woman wants to throw herself into a man's arms...but a man wants to throw himself between a woman's legs.

Another misunderstanding:—A man enjoys a woman. But a woman doesn't want to be enjoyed; she wants to be appreciated.

A further misunderstanding:—She says, "How do I love thee? Let me count the ways." He says, "How do I love thee? Let me count the times."

Still further misunderstandings:—For her, love is existence; for him, instances. For her, immersion; for him, repetition. For her, feeling; for him, doing. For her, a relationship; for him, relations. In all, she wants more love; he wants love more often.

. . .Wait a minute. Am I making men look better than they really are?

270

Some crucial distinctions:—

Whether a woman helps a man to stand tall, or whether she just props him up. Whether a woman urges a man forward, or pushes him down.

Whether she draws out his best, or sucks out his all.

There is a subtle difference between the repose following gratification and the inertia following emasculation. A woman may make a man more, or she may reduce him to nothing.

These are absolute alternatives, even if we sometimes have difficulty distinguishing between those who have found fulfillment and those who have merely undergone the operation. Highly spiritualized men act overtly like eunuchs. And even they might not understand the difference.

271

In pursuing my theme, the relations between the sexes, I am only considering the typical. The modern American couple, for example. I remember the prototype from my generation, namely, the hippie couple of the Sixties:

She looked like a minister's daughter who liberated herself from repression (but not, we were convinced, from its effects). Bespectacled in the gold-rimmed style of grandma's time, she gazed out upon the world with a smug intellectuality that was assertive, contemptuous, and oh-so-equal.

Disdaining cosmetics, she was plain, plain, plain in a contrived affectation of plainness. She dressed and acted like the country yokel who had quit the land to become a warehouse janitor in the city. And, yes, she allowed herself to become unkempt and dirty. So much more natural, she thought.

The shehippie was cerebralized, male-mimicking, willful, contentious,—in short, a woman as castrated man, exemplar of Plato's nasty definition, if ever there was one.

Most and worst of all, this protoliberated young woman, riding forth brandishing the banners of free love and abortion, was totally sexless. An active and promiscuous fornicator, certainly. But an animal female woman who warmed to her man and took sex to heart? Never. She had no sex, she had no heart. Her body was an automaton of flat-chested mechanico-cerebrality. Lady Macbeth was her patron saint, but not her equal.

Having finished my lyric and litany to the lady, I'll now consider her consort. The most that can be said about him is that he was in matching costume overalls. He seemed to have once been smitten by the image in Grant Wood's *American Gothic* and henceforth took the man in the painting as mirror.

The hehippie attempted to project something of the sagacity of the prophets, although his knowledge of the Old Testament was akin to the screwball exegesis of the Jehovah's Witnesses. Still, he could stroke his beard to dislodge a concealed louse, if not to elicit any canticles or proverbs. Why he would want to emulate an ancient Jew is not clear. Perhaps he imitated the ideocentric life, the detachedness, of the ancient

Hebrews. Like the special people, he a special person.

A reformer, he was ambitious to scheme a reorganization of the world, though he didn't understand it or belong to it. An ideological activist to compensate for being a sexual passivist (by comparison to his self- and sex-assertive sidekick). Sex had gone to his head, and his head had gone to hormonal politics. Presto, a radical idealist! He wanted to reform the world, he who had lost his own manhood to that freak-female monster at his side.

Their true devotion being to narcotic self-indulgence, the hippie couple were morally concave and spiritually empty, all the rattling and exhibition of their righteous revolutionarian idealism notwithstanding. They were just too stoned to get up and out into the world to reform it.

And the relationship between them, as man and woman? An ambivalent transsexual one, the forerunner of the current relatedness between the sexes.

As types, the Sixties' hippies were caricatures of character. In reality, the shrew was a meek, library-mongering minister's daughter still. And the Jew was a Philistine. Yes, I remember the prototype of the modern couple,—Mouse and the Messiah.

272

A *marriage of the minds* makes estranged bedfellows.

273

Woman-will:—Now, there's a new hyphenated dirty word for my vocabulary. I got it from D.H. Lawrence, and I would have passed it by, except for the fact that I am in daily contact with a young female who is woman-will incarnate. She is an embodiment, a veritable epitome, of D.H. Lawrence's identified type. Her assertiveness makes me want to run and hide behind Lao-tzu's skirts.

She is my avian aggravation. Her head is always turned askew, so that she regards everyone monocularly, in true eagle fashion. She curls what little lip she has in a twist of general contempt. It is no lip, but a beak, rather. Her tongue must be like that of the woodpecker, lancelike and spiny to pierce my brain and gouge out all my cerebral ants. And her speech is a dry squawking crackle, as if she were still in the process of swallowing some of her victims' bones. Woe to me, whenever I try to get oral or verbal with her.

Oh, and so sure of herself. I have never heard such a ceaseless striking-off of flinty sentences of adamant affirmation. She preludes all her opinions with "Of course", then manages to follow up such egotistic impertinence with one banal truism after another. Shallow profundity!

She plays the oracle, *ex cathedra*, or from the eyrie, rather. "Screech! Squawk! Caw-caw!"—That is the revelation from that griffin, that feathered gargoyle.

The birdbrain idiocy of superficial intelligence:—That is what that vulture impersonating an owl has demonstrated to me. She bites spectacularly, but bite is all there is to her. Her head is all eye and beak; there is no mind behind. But she is as cocksure as an eaglemaniac, that impertinent hen who makes mockery of the role of rooster. There is no brood-spot on her breast.

She knows it all, she is superior to all, she deserves everything, she will do whatever she wants, and she will get you if you don't watch out. I see her talons spasmodically clutching the air, clawfully sharpening themselves in preparation for the phallectomy.

Ah, this rancor in my soul, it doesn't become me. But she irritates me so, like a gonococcus; no, a gynococcus. And to think that I actually once desired her! From a distance, of course. With proximity, my desire has been transmuted into funk.

I confess my helplessness and utter exasperation in dealing with her. She has beaten me down with her woman-will, willed my own will out of me, and hung me limp from a limb, like a dead rabbit. I surrender!

Well, I'm a traditionalist, anyway. I prefer the old-fashioned woman-as-sphinx to this new, modern woman-as-harpy.

274

What ambiguity and irony have befallen the word *mistress* during the evolution of its meaning.

Mistress once meant a genteel lady of the house, then lover and kept woman, and now it denotes a dog owner.

If the women's liberationists have their way, the word *wife* will undergo the exact same semantic progression. They have already undermined the first definition by polemicizing against *of the house* and scoffing at the ideal of *lady*. And they are determined to be not kept, but keeper. Once those warped reformers have fully disposed of the second definition of *wife*, I needn't exercise much imagination to foresee the next stage in women's *emancipation* and men's subjugation.

Ah-ooo!, you modern mistresses, you won't collar-and-leash me. We last few wild wolves that have resisted the taming by social enlightenment will not go the way of the dogs. If captured, we'll snarl, bite the hand of the mistress, and leap over the kennel walls back to freedom.

Woe to the woman of the third stage of definition of the word *wife*! In trying to make a docile house pet, she will have roused up the man's better instincts. Then, maybe, after a brief bout of growling and snarling and scuffling, male and female human animals can settle down to dynamic polarity and gender complementarity once again.

275

In the Battle between the Sexes, a woman may lose the battle, a man may lose his sex.

276

How the attrition of the years dilutes a man's ambition toward women. A young man's inordinate self-estimate gradually diminishes, until, facing middle age, the man tries harder and harder, believing in himself less and less. Once he was confident of conquest; now he would settle for, would be most grateful for, mere acceptance. Meanwhile, he can barely hold his own in dealing with a woman.

Women learned long ago that the battle plan for the defeat of men is to withhold themselves. (In that respect, prostitutes practice treason against womankind.) A lot of woman's strategy for controlling man has been in the spirit of *Lysistrata*, that is, withholding as a tactic.

Thank God our modern liberated women bang their bodies, as well as their heads, against men. Women have dropped their most formidable weapon to skirmish with men on men's terms.

A woman overcomes by withdrawing and withholding. Lao-tzu and the author of *Lysistrata*, old Aristophanes, knew that.

On behalf of manlykind, I breathe a sigh of relief that women have been converted to manly sexual looseness. Chronic privation is bad enough, but one can get used to it. Sudden deprivation due to female withholding is a worse, a more calculated, a more humiliating scourge upon the male. It is better never to have loved at all than to have loved and have had love taken away, which sentiment I assert in the face of the

Romantic happy and self-indulgent sufferers. Oh, St. Tantalus, deliver us!

One distant day, long ago in some prehistoric age, woman discovered power through withholding. On that same day man discovered loneliness. Modern woman, careless in promiscuity, has been drawn away from her most effective tactic against man. Pray she doesn't come to her senses and rediscover withholding, for, if she does, man will have to relearn loneliness.

277

Traditional woman said to man, "Give me love, then I will give you sex."

Modern woman gives sex, then pleads, "Please give me love."

Women seem to have utterly abandoned their immemorially successful strategy. Their bargaining leverage now lost, women's new generosity will ultimately prove self-defeating.

A Mediterranean analogy, inspired by this Italian environment:—Once a man has gorged freely on the grapes, he loses motivation to cultivate the fruiting vine.

278

A shrewd fellow I know used to insist upon an absolute law of inverse relationship between capability and volubility, or, to put it more simply, between what was done and what is bragged about. Those who weave tales of their intoxicative accomplishments, he argued, are usually easy-puking short-hitters.

My friend provided me with one of the most valid little formulas for the interpretation of human behavior that I have ever found. I always listen to how much a person says about something, in order to gauge how little is his experience and accomplishment.

I took up my friend's theme, but, raising the tone of the conversation, I told him, "There are two distinct classes,—lovers and those who talk about loving."

Ah, those silent and smiling types, how I envy them! The sigh of remembered experience conveys more truth than the talk-on of words or the write-on of pages.

Verbum non est factum, factum non est verbum, to say it in Latin, here in Rome.

279

The lecher's morality:—A *good* woman does what she shouldn't. A *bad* woman doesn't do what she shouldn't.

The lecher himself, of course, always does what he wants.

The laugh against the lecher is that this man who uses sex is used by sex. He shouts, "Giddy-up!", but the ass wields the whip.

280

The British think that sex is a sneeze; the French, that it is an invigorating deep breath; the Italians, that it is a smacking of the tongue; the Americans, that it is a belch and grunt.

281

The sexual relationship seems to follow the same course as influenza:—At first, high fever and a fast pulse; then, a drop in temperature and dull aches in various parts of the body; and, at last, a sigh and a few sniffles.

282

Before sexual intercourse, the boy in the man plays exhibitionist to please his mother, but he only succeeds in embarrassing his daughter. (Freudian paradox.)

283

In sexual intercourse, the man exclaims, "I got it!"

In sexual intercourse, the woman exclaims, "I got him!"

284

Man and woman, once the *yin* and *yang* of the universe, the systole and diastole of earth's heartbeat, God's greatest complementary creations, (indeed images of the Creator Himself), immortal souls second only to the angels, dual embodiment of God's love, the creatures with the most potential for participating in God's creative power have become…mere things that bump each other in the night.

285

"A Writer's Dilemma"

I am at a very difficult stage in life right now,— too old to be a *boy wonder* and too young to be a *dirty old man*.

286

Another awkward stage, a too-late, too-early conjunction in my life:—I am an aging lover but still a fledgling writer. Oh, exasperation! Am I now trying to find the words for that which I am no longer capable of, or even that which I can no longer remember? What, *me*, impotent, senile, and vocationally inept?

. . . I am on the brink of an epigram. Could it be that writing is the "fun of the done redone"? Or "the issue in tissue of the seeds of sex"? Or "the salute of the sad to the joys of boys"? Or how about "a word from the wise to the sensually sufficient"?

I am being flippant, of course; but the epigram is only a little better sort of pun, anyway. One must find means to retain one's libidinal vigor. Flippancy forestalls floppancy. Wit is one-upmanship, and I'm one man who wants to keep up his upship.

Up and forward! should be my motto, in life, in love, and in literary lechery.

Am I too gray for bodies and too green for literature? Nonsense! The phallic pen is mightier than the bored and will persevere through periods of fallow disheartedness and dismindedness. The libido-literary life-lover is a vital animal. No matter how many times he has been laid low, he always manages to get back up, get it up (his pen, I mean), get on with it, and generally get going again. *"Exegi monumentum aere perennius,"* a monument more enduring than bronze, he exclaims, contemplating his book...and his body.

I may not yet have written THE BOOK, but I have sprinkled a few homuncular phrases here and there. Because of that, the women, rather than the men, have lionized me; I refer to personal testimonials and such. What is the cold cash of the Nobel Prize for Literature compared to the warm smiles, the flushed and glowing faces of all those feline females? There are, after all, quite different contexts in which the enthusiastic shouts of *"Bravo! Bis!"* are heard, as, for example, between sheets of manuscript, or, more simply, between sheets.

The continuity of consciousness in my life has been provided by the thematic thread of *instinct*, that single strand of perfervid preoccupation. A hell of a lot of wishful thinking over a hell of a long time, to be sure. I am evidently one of those panerotic maniacs who occur from time to time, satyrs who set their sexual psyches against the civilized world.

I am a mystic, I am a libertine, effulgent and decadent at the same time. I am a good and a bad fused into an actual. It is all variable process and paradox, and it is all me.

Oh, this life is long and I am already tired, but I have not yet begun to live. I have sinned, *mea gaudia, mea gaudia, mea maxima gaudia,* and I hope to have many opportunities to sin again.

The Sacred is the path to the Profane and vice versa; I am a two-way commuter on that line. And there is no philosopher more grave than the buffoon.

I am more or less convinced of my greater or lesser conviction, but I hope to ever suspend judgment on myself. Let he who is without stones commit the first sin, or something like that.

. . .What am I writing? Damn, drunk again!

287

My written word is the corpse of a spent impulse.

288

That rumor—about me making love, then leaping out of bed to take notes—is a lie and a slander and a defamation of my character!

289

I made love to her, the woman I loved, three times that night.

I gave my all, of passion, of love. A fiery first time. Then a second hot and flowing time. Briefly recovered, then a wet and warm third time. Three times I had spent the all of myself, poured out my all into her, the woman I loved.

As we slept, I dreamt, and in my dream I saw a vision of an alluring stranger, an anonymous unknown female, a libidinal phantom. As I approached her, my lust surged. She threw off her clothes, I rose up to her exposed receptivity, throbbing at the brink. . .

I awoke and sat up straight.

I fell back to the pillow, where I saw in the dim light the head of the woman I loved, she asleep beside me. Her presence startled me, as if *she* were the stranger, an intruder into my private intimacy with the female phantom of the dream.

I lay between two women, then, each reaching out for me. My dayawake love and my phantasmagorical dream-lover, each trying to wring me dry, but each failing to distract my attention away from the other.

I sat up again in bed, raised my naked arms to heaven and cried out, "What is enough? There's never enough! Not even love is enough!"

I went back to sleep with apprehension. And I never confessed my infidelity to the woman I loved.

But the next time I made love to her, gave my all to her, I felt the fleeting presence of the phantom female of my dream hovering over me, licking her lips, waiting her turn.

290

Love is my guardian angel. She stands at my right shoulder smiling.

Lust is my guardian devil. He sits on my left shoulder with a big grin on his face.

Surges in the Flow

[Reassurance to readers: The following is erotic but refined.]

291

Culture is for rainy days and winter. We would never have become enculturated, if bad weather had not forced us inside and, so, within ourselves. Once we walked in the sunshine as naked and unselfconscious as the other animals. Then a chill wind blew in. We shivered, got dressed, and, confined to shelter, had nothing else to do but think it all over. It was an ill wind indeed that brought the birth of rumination.

A causative factor in the evolution of culture, from cave painting to nihilism, has been bad weather. Culture is the cumulative doodling of our confinement.

If the climate everywhere had remained Edenal, mankind would have continued to live the life of the body, of instinct, of thoughtfree sensuality, like the Polynesians. However, inclement weather has, in most parts of the globe, forced us in upon ourselves. We have had to cover our bodies, thus becoming desensitized, and we must live a good part of our time in an artificial indoors environment, clothed and sheltered against the natural elements.

Having cast those molds of clothing and housing, man then recast his own mold, his body. He fabricated an occupant *soul* for himself. Alas, the loss of animal simplicity! Enter religion, followed by a haunting host of intellectual scourges. "Naked and ashamed".

Judge our perversity and the reversal of natural sensitivity by the psychological fact that we feel comfortable when clothed, but ill at ease when naked. Bad weather then, bad conscience now.

I could enumerate, and elaborate on, all the advantages of civilization. Still, something within me remains unconvinced. I think it is called *instinct*. "Look what civilization has done to me!," it protests. "Ah, yes...," I admit, "but what about *sublimation*?" "Emasculation!", instinct scoffs.

The pity of culture is that we had to give up so much of natural life in the process of making our physical living more secure. Encultured man is a worse animal better off. Our bodies no longer shiver, but our minds do.

I think we have inklings of what has happened to us, when warming weather seduces us to relapse into simple physiological sensuality. *Spring fever* is a resurgence of our animal energetics. When THE DAY beckons, who wants culture then?

Rome, like any other place, is actually only a *hibernopolis*, a wintering-place. During these fresh vernal days, I feel an urge to shed my clothes, and culture, and Rome, to plunge back into somatic animal vitality in the midst of Nature. Good weather arouses the good body. In spring, we discover that we are alive, after all. Against that transcendent fact, culture is a rude impertinence.

292

Awakening, arousal. This is spring, season of physiological and spiritual resuscitation. Apparently I have not aged so much as to be insensitive to the stirrings of spring sensations. I felt them today, even in the culture-cloister of the city of Rome.

Springtime effects the regeneration of animality within us. Perhaps it is in the simple act of shedding some of our clothing to respond to the warming days that we annually rediscover our animal sensitivity. Spring entices us toward more and more nakedness, more self-exposure, more sensuality. The rite of spring is a strip. We drop winter clothes and winter insulation, leaping in ecstatic exultation, naked and tingling.

I feel this changing season as a tactile experience, through all my pores. The breezes of spring chill and warm my skin in alternate caprices. I breathe in the new spring air and feel lightheaded. I become giddy with my reinvigoration.

Springtime is the season of *eros*, as the Romantic poets recognize in their symbolic effusions on budding blossoms, blooming flowers, and mating birds. The celibacy of winter is left behind. All life becomes erotically charged.

Lying face down in the Villa Adriana at Tivoli, I inhale the wafted aromas of thawed living earth and raw grass. Deep inner stirrings respond with the mystical intensity of the mating urge. Something within remains cyclical.

Ah, to be in love in spring! To complement the tactile stimulations of the weather with surging visceral seething. . . Would we not swoon in a delirium of the intensity of our living?

By *love* I mean not the bland, handholding sentimentality of the Romantics, but, rather, the charged fury of surging blood and seed and sex, the male and female impelled into each other with the thrust of their magnetic polarity. In this love, the utter nakedness of naked interpenetration!

The sensory experience of spring and the visceral experience of human love:—Won't we wholly recover our primordial animal vitality, as those two forces fire us from without and within? The earth touches a man, and he touches a woman. All three members of that triad leap into life at the contact!

293

Do adults lose the season of summer in their lives? They persist in plodding and plotting with their usual hibernal grimness all through the months when every other living being in Nature lies languid and loving itself in the sun.

The brilliance of summer light bids us to stop doing and simply look. The intensity of summer heat lulls our thinking and enkindles our capacity for feeling.

Why do we resist such inducements to renewal? What madmen and blasphemers are those who spite the summer by clinging fast to the stifling garments of their winter vices.

I remember how, as a schoolboy, I used to anticipate the arrival of summer with a longing more powerful than most other passions I have felt since. I sighed and tingled all through suspenseful springtime with a disturbing restlessness, a pubescent pain and expectancy, an unquenchable craving for consummation between my body and all Nature. Children are pagans and pantheists; their instincts are sound.

When school finished at last, I would carry my books home, tear them to shreds, and throw them into the trash in the excitement of sudden liberation. No more classroom confinement. I would whoop and leap off into the Dionysian vitality of outdoor summer living.

—(I hope to repeat such a summer orgy all my life. I never write during the summer; that would be unwholesome.)—

How many painful May and June days I spent as an adolescent, deluded in thinking that I wanted love and sex. My genital stirrings were only localized spasms, compared to my wholly overwhelming passion for immersion in Life and Nature.

Summer makes a Transcendentalist out of anyone who is still at all sensitive. Its alchemy is the transmutation of body into spirit. Thoreau was, in his own way, as sensuous as Whitman.

294

Autumn is the least sensual of the seasons. Those days of dimming light, when all the world seems dry and dying, make one pensive and introspective. Our awareness becomes philosophical, rather than physiological. We age abruptly; our senses turn senile. Who thinks of sex in autumn?

The nymphs and satyrs shiver in despondency and reluctantly clothe themselves against the coming winter. Every fluid in Nature—water and blood, froth and sperm—turns sluggish in the desiccate air. In the autumnal aura of stale, ebbing life, the current of sex ceases its flow or diminishes to a mere trickle.

To those stags who are heedless of impending winter, autumn is the rutting season, the new chill but whetting their lust and aggressiveness. But man, the apprehensive animal, anticipates the winter gloom before it is upon him. He gradually withdraws into his innermost organs and lets his skin take on a barklike insensitivity. It's autumn. Winter is coming. Bundle up!

Outdoor sex in that season, any foolhardy nakedness, any spending of one's body warmth in steaming passion, risks a fatal chill. Autumn is the season, not for acts of erotic expenditure, but for self-preservative hoarding of one's own heat.

How different are the images of sexing in the bright, wet vernal bed of new green grass, compared to sexing on the dry, crusty pile of dead brown leaves. Sex in spring comes with the spontaneity of impulses participating in the overpowering enthusiasm of Nature's orgy. Sex in autumn is a jangled, out-of-tune cacophony.

As spring is a coming-to-life, so autumn is a receding from life. Hedonist Nature has turned Puritan and frowns on late-season lovers.

During autumn, inspiration dried up, the Romantic poets stop writing verses and reread the verses they wrote in springtime. Libidinous lovers, meanwhile, reminisce in nostalgia about their erotic mischief and adventures of the past spring; desire droops, and lovers take solace in memory. What sighs, what sadness there is in the sexlessness of autumn!

Where is the man of inextinguishable passion, the artist potent enough to libidinize the autumn season and put the torch to Nature and to desire? Imagine such a vibrant, unquenchable spirit, a tireless year-round lover. His work-of-art-and-instinct would be, let's say, the tale of a honeymoon in autumn. Think of the incongruity of that idea,—a honeymoon in autumn. The passion of new sex amidst the dullness and torpor of a moribund Nature. Only a great lover and wizard of words could achieve such a masterpiece of literary vitality. Has it ever been done? Could it be done?

295

Randy on a rainy afternoon. The dullness and drizzle outside are hypnotic, inducing a heavy-lidded sensual sleepiness in me. There is no place to go and nothing to do. I am full-bellied and drowsy. I lapse into the slow-rhythmed breathing of sleep.

What better way to while away the rainy hours of life than naked in bed making love and then sleeping until supper? But she is not here now. I am alone looking out at the tedium of rain. I feel an ache, the plaintive stirring of insistent instinct.

The rain is becoming as constant as desire. And the ache is as steady as the rain.

296

Sex in the sunshine! This is the hot summer of youth and sensuality. The sun is a satyr who strokes the sensitivity of our exposed nakedness with lascivious touches. The woman and I warm, turn drowsy and carnal under his caresses.

As we are further enkindled, our sultry languor becomes burning arousal. Blood flows like a stream of hot, viscous lava, massing itself and rising up from the innermost depths of our bodies. A staccato series of primordial sensations tantalizes and charges us with ever mounting tension.

The woman and I begin to ooze and flow in lubrication of each other, transpiration, sweat and saliva. All the air and the surface of our skins have become tropically heavy, humid, teeming, and luxurious.

The flowing fires of our blood intermingle, and the jungle beat of pulsations pounds out its frantic rhythm in the barbaric madness of passion. We exhaust ourselves into each other, thrusting the inflamed parts into the fire of the forge, assaulting each other's naked openness with the spasmodic thumps of pleasure and pain.

We interpenetrate in fiery fusion, then abruptly explode apart, shattering the stillness of the African summer. . .

The fire and boiling water trail away in smoke and steam. The flood current ebbs, the deafening crescendo is followed by a *pianissimo* pitter-patter. We become drowsy.

And, after a sigh for sex and this summer, we sleep.

297

A verse fragment of a seduction lyric, written in the youth of my youth:

Wash your mouth.
Rinse off all his kisses from your lips.
Scrub your hands 'til all the warmth of his is gone.
Stand naked in the shower; let running water carry away
Every trace of him left by embrace or touch.
Cleanse your mind of every memory of him.
After that total ablution, pure and clean in all your being,
Cover your nakedness in clothes unseen by him.
Then come to me.

298

Ten years have passed between my *Sensations* and this *Instinct*, one third of my life, yet each work is the statement of the same theme, namely, that natural instinct is the way to transcendence, that the lowest of the organic approaches the highest of the spiritual.

Instinct is an ever-present motif in my mind; that motif sounds irrespective of time, place, or circumstance. The passage of time has refined my articulation, but it has not modified my conviction. I haven't matured out of the wistful, wishful thinking of *Sensations*, but my thinking has matured in me. Long and laborious is the tortuous course of return to the first insights of our youth. Will I spend my entire life continually rewriting the same text?

Now, all this is not to say that I have spent the past decade in a static existential vacuum. Far from it. I have had, in fact, nothing less than experiential verification of a hypothesis first formed in the naïveté of virginal ignorance. When the idea was made flesh, I became more sane and healthy and vital than I had ever been before or have been since.

Nothing reinforces a fantasy like its actual realization. If it weren't for *her*, for that experience with her, I may have proceeded to the life-denying cerebralism I now so thoroughly abhor. I no longer write from my head.

Once you have touched Life, you will never lose touch with it. So, while in *Sensations* I imagined and rhapsodized on a desired but unknown experience, as I write this *Instinct* I know what I am talking about. Before, I dreamt. Now I live in the dream. And my writing is only the vaguest suggestion of the richness of my life-experience.

Animal instinct is not something that must be overcome. Instinct must be come back to, come down to. The path to the healthy highest in us opens upon acceptance of, embrace of, the healthy lowest within us.

Elemental organic animal instinct, the touch of Life itself, is the portal to spirituality. Both my writing and my living are unfolding as elaboration of that idea, simple as it is. Despite privation and frustration, that deep intuition abides within me. My intuition is *eros*, the instinct toward health and liveliness. That little idea is, at times, the only thing that sustains me, the only good idea I have ever had.

299

My teaching is the song of *eros*. How I lick and lap and love my students with my words!

I step out of loneliness into a tryst with my assembled lovers. They await me wide-eyed, receptive to my verbal blandishments. In tenderness and compassion, I enfold them. They have come to learn language, but what I want to teach them is loving.

This teaching-and-learning is not a mere mechanical antiphon of words. It is an amorous interplay, a wooing, a fondling, an intimacy between the teacher and his students. We all warm to one another in sympathy, as we warm to human communication in the English language.

Yes, my teaching is a labor of love, indeed a labor of sex. My spoken words are not data from the cranium; they are pulses from my blood, breaths from my lungs, seed from my loins. I was hired to impart knowledge, to be confidential, which I do, which I am. Beyond that I disseminate myself. I get intimate.

My female students sense that I am more than a hired valve that pours out grammar and vocabulary. They feel the effusion of my male mystique, they look at me with the hushed awe that the naked woman feels for the naked man. I have seduced them. They are in love with me.

They express their erotic nexus by the zeal with which they study; woman wants to please her man. They give an answer, then look up to me, pleading the look-back of male approval. Beneath the subterfuge of the study of language, we love one another.

Francesca and Costanza have responded.

The male students in my class do not take part in this tensioned attraction. I doubt they even sense the erotic electricity in the classroom, but, amidst the stimulated women, they too are stimulated, if only to learn.

My best, most fecund class groups are those composed mostly of women. Those classes are charged with the fertile dynamism of sexual attraction. Classes in which men predominate are anarchic; I struggle against other asserted masculinity in a fruitless clash. I prefer my harem.

Teaching may be the only companionship available to the lonely. A solitary man is sought to give of himself and of the substance earned from solitude. By teaching, he can feel the consolation of human inclusion. The heretofore distant and unreachable women come to him, eager and receptive. Then, surely, the teacher must love them.

The mind is the deep well, and the mouth the font of the verbal stream of *eros*. My classroom is a private chamber for an act of love. It is all sublimated sexuality. Teaching is touching.

300

I have never been to a place more adorned with beautiful girls and women than this city of Rome. They surround me with an exquisite feminine elegance of sculpted heads, distinctive aquiline noses, sunshine skin, and the bodies of love-goddesses. When they swirl by me as we pass in the streets, I nearly faint in a dizzy swoon. I stop, and stare, and sigh in delirious appreciation.

Yet, the men mingle among the women as with the city's monuments, with an air of inattentive familiarity. The Roman has become inured to the beauty that surrounds him.

301

So real was Proserpine in her voluptuous nakedness, her flesh soft and yielding to the clutches of the ravisher—(Bernini's sculpture in the Borghese Gallery)—that I almost leapt upon the pedestal in a libidinal frenzy to do battle with

Pluto himself for possession, so aroused was I by the dynamism of desire and resistance, carved by Bernini into the swirling forms of struggle.

I respond at a deeper human depth to the sculpture of Gianlorenzo Bernini than I do to that of Michelangelo, our other Roman titan. Bernini sculpts carnality and sensuality. When I approach Bernini's pieces, I get all stirred up, I get physically involved. Very different from Michelangelo's work, which merely induces a detached aesthetic reverence, almost an intimidation. Albeit that my mind may assume a classical pose, the senses of my body are drawn to the Baroque.

Michelangelo is cosmic, of course, but Bernini is organic. If the first is suprahuman, the second is panhuman. When I experience the sculptures of Bernini, I am seduced to the physical, I want physical consummation. Congenial paganism!

"Oh, beautiful body, what are we to each other? How can I relate to you? I want you!" So exclaims the ecstatic visual lover of corporal sculpture.

302

I have come to Florence to see a man and a woman. My interest in them is philosomatic. The man is Michelangelo's *David*, the naked male colossus. As I approached him in the Accadèmia Gallery, I found his awesome masculinity to be even more imposing than I remembered it from our first encounter seven years ago. The Florentine woman is Sandro Botticelli's *Venus*, the ever-alluring form of idealized femininity.

David and *Venus*,—idolatrous creations out of the wellsprings of two very different types of erotic genius, yet each work, in its own way, an apotheosis of the human body.

Nakedness always beckons, and it is naïve to think that it beckons only to be admired from a distance. Our response to a nude is a complex process of higher and lower attractions. The nude whispers, "Look at me, touch me, embrace me." As we respond to the nude in art, don't we sense beneath the educated aestheticism of detached admiration a craving, a carnal lust toward, almost a desire to incorporate the beauty of the ideal body?

We identify our own body with the ideal nude and are envious. We offer our own body as a mate to the nude and are lustful. Ultimately, we desire to be and become the body of the ideal by consuming it. That is hunger...for the flesh of the nude. Our appreciation is a veritable cannibalism.

There is a deep psychological significance in the idiomatic expression we use in effusive praise for a body we love,—"I could eat you up!" Botticelli's *Venus*, then, stands not upon a half-shell, but, rather, on a serving dish, and delectable indeed.

303

The *sleeping statues*:—How they entice me to tender approach. What fascination I feel for the lax and unconscious forms hammered out of the adamant marble.

I am thinking once again about the classical sculptures of recumbent and unconscious human bodies:—The various versions of the Sleeping Hermaphrodite, Sleeping Ariadne, Endymion, the statuettes of children nodding on the brink of dozing off, the drunken satyrs staggered back and lapsing into obliviousness; or of the depiction of the sleeplike overcoming that is death, as we see it in the famous *Dying Gaul* and in the heads of dying soldiers and gladiators. Sleep and death. We as spectators draw near and are stilled.

Why?

We first confront a paradox, that of the relation of the subject matter to the material. Why did the sculptors choose the softness of sleep as a theme to be rendered in the hard monumentality of chiseled marble? One would think that sculpture in stone is a suitable medium only for depicting the solidity of corporality, as in muscular athletes and voluptuous female nudes.

Hard marble for the hard facts of life and art. There *are* many examples of such depiction in classical sculpture. Every Apollo and Venus is a full and formidable solid physical presence. In *kouros* and *koré* the human body is hardened, marbleized, monumentalized.

In contrast to the artistic tradition of sculpture as a rigidification of the body, a *rigor vitae*, we encounter these sleeping statues. Why did sculptors stray from their monumentalizing bias toward the body and drift into the lyricism and laxity of sleep and even death? How can we account for the metamorphosis of marble into Morpheus?

The material seems a most inappropriate medium for the motif. Nonetheless, the sculptors attacked the rock and whacked away, chipping out, then smoothing off the curves and lapses of sleep and death.

The dynamic activism of carved images of assertive strength, as in Jupiter or Hercules, was complemented by an atavistic passivism. The ancient world was becoming tired out by its excesses. If consciousness is too stressful, then back into the oblivion of sleep or into that selfless nothingness that preceded our personal consciousness and will sweep around and inevitably swallow us up again. These statues express a longing for sleep and death.

And what about our modern response? We too find the sensuality of sleep alluring. Is sleep the wish-fulfillment of our wakefulness? Do we want a blissful lapse into the *alpha* and *omega* of oblivion? Is ultimate unconsciousness the deepest yearning of our consciousness?

"Come, sleep with me," Hermaphrodite urges. How do we respond to, or fend off, the seductive call of sleep and death?

304

As I stood watching the lax and languid form of the Sleeping Hermaphrodite in the National Roman Museum yesterday, I was startled to see the marble torso rise and fall in a respiratory rhythm.

For a few seconds the bare stone became flesh and the core of the rock softened into the warm organic expansiveness of lungs. The hewn statue was transfigured into a living human body. Hermaphrodite was alive and breathing!

That fleeting hallucination was caused by my own respiration, which, swelling my chest, made my head and eyes rise and fall slightly as I stared fixedly at Hermaphrodite. My eyes externalized that movement and projected it onto the recumbent form.

By an act of unconscious wish-fulfillment, I breathed life into the inanimate sculpture. Hermaphrodite quickened. At that, I wanted to reach out to touch the warm flesh. How thrilled I was!

I have experienced that visual misperception a few other times while looking at classical corporal sculpture. Each time my error enlivened the figure. I think I have discovered a perceptual stimulus for the myth of Pygmalion.

Classical sculpture, the embodiment of the philosomatic ideal, beckons us to an erotic involvement. My body loves the ideal body. Oh, if only lithic material were human flesh!

Today, I am back in Florence, where there is another Sleeping Hermaphrodite, in the Uffizi. Heavy red curtains darken the room in which Hermaphrodite lies. I stood near, silently, so as not to disturb that sleep. I gazed tenderly at the gentle curves of the lower back and thighs, as they gleamed a reflection of the muffled light.

Hermaphrodite was alive, as woman, man, child, human being in totality, sleeping in a sweet unconsciousness, unknowingly drawing us with the exquisitely beautiful simplicity of carnal sensuality.

Whether Hermaphrodite breathed or I breathed or both of us breathed, I know not. But there was between us a breath of love, a mystic and exhilarating deep breath of love for the body.

Hermaphrodite and I are but two emanations of a single god,—Eros.

305

(At the Capitoline Museums.)

While admiring the images of the human body crafted in rock and marble, I was not insensitive to other statuesque presences around me. I found the females in the flesh more alluring than those on exhibit; even the Capitoline Venus enticed me only in so far as cold stone suggested warm flesh. My aesthetics was mersed with sexthetics.

Nature always calls us back from culture. Genitality permeates the spirit.

The museum's a fine and public place,
But none, I think, do there embrace.

306

My body remains unconvinced of my mind's spiritual pretensions.

"I shall love," says my mind proudly.

"But I lust, and you know it," my body responds in rebuttal.

Animal-corporal smolders every moment, inflaming ambitious attempts at cool spirituality.

307

The heady intoxication of the smell of her sweat smothered beneath heavy perfume!...I swoon as I catch the faint, wafted aroma of muffled femaleness. Memory abides in all the senses, and oh the sensory privation of the deprived! Taunting, tantalizing sights and sounds and that scent. Breathing, sniffing, seeking the scent...of the female!

308

I am ever poised on a fulcrum. Although I try to maintain balance, I am pushed by my centrifugal drive, pulled by another's centripetal allure. Efferent surges flow from me in vectors, out to the closed circle terminus of my surroundings. At the same time, the rays of afferent temptations appeal to me from all sides, targeting my body.

That is the organic tension of sexual feeling: I, lusting indiscriminately outward toward all, toward nothing; I, being indiscriminately taunted by the alluring female forms around me. A seducer may himself be seduced.

A man's body is churned to turbulence by the relentless inner and outer forces. Need pounding within, allure beckoning from without...and a staggering and struggle for precarious balance and control. Only a small extra surge of drive or a slightly more intense temptation can cause a fall.

The mind's awareness of the body's insistent need, that sensory introspection, intensifies to full obsession. Closed eyes look down into the black, irresistible demands of drive. But to escape into open-eyed awareness of others only exposes a man to the force of allure. Our will is always at war with our instinct.

Human need is more insistent than there could ever be opportunities for its satisfaction, so, sex can make us predatory. But if we can cultivate a self-compassionate patience, if we can wait until true love herself welcomes us, then do body and soul both find their fulfillment.

Meanwhile, a man is always at the tipping point; or, said otherwise, tied in the middle of a tug-o'-war between impelling drive and seductive allure. An exquisite affliction, that poignance of our instinctual lives!

Despite the Christian campaign to extirpate instinct, we realize that it is the opposing push-pull tensions of our sexuality that stimulate our liveliness. Erotic feeling is painful, agonizing, but vitalizing.

We live in suspense. I myself stand poised on the fulcrum, contesting the forces of drive and allure. With what slight nudge, whether from within or without, do I tumble...or do I soar!

309

I still love those who have let me go. Can I ever accept that once there was a woman who loved me—more than life she loved me—, but that now for whom I am a past and a forgotten?

The desire for love and sex of someone who has known both,—that erotic nostalgia. I yearn. And my yearning yearns.

Memories by day, retrospective dreams by night...So runs the course of consciousness, the course of desire, in the now-nonloving lover who remembers.

310

Desire, craving for other, loses this, utterly, until, nothing gained and all lost, desire only desires itself.

311

There are three ways of dealing with desire: Extinguish it, control it, or indulge it.

From extinguishment comes Christian sanctity; from control, restlessness; from indulgence, renewed ever-insatiable desire!

312

"The curious sympathy one feels when feeling with the hand the naked meat of the body. . ."

Yes, Walt, the touch is sympathy itself.

A woman, just having given birth, weary of her labor, looks down upon her raw infant in her arms, and, with trembling fingers, touches it upon its cheek with two fingertips, then drops the length of her fingers along the infant's face, until the entire warm palm of her hand cradles the child's head. And, inside that head, awareness dawns.

The first touch of our lives, that extension of loving maternal sympathy, awakens our consciousness. Being born, the child is a physiological organism merely. Having been touched, it becomes a human being.

The touch stimulates awareness of the self, awareness of the other, and mutual sympathy between the self and the other. The child that is touched, caressed, and hugged is a loved child, and so discovers what love is, first receiving love, then reciprocating love, at last offering love. The touch is a language of love more eloquent and sincere than any words or music of voice. Our very love of life itself comes from touching and being touched.

As the child grows up, the parents reduce the frequency and intensity of their touches, caresses, and embraces. That withdrawal is one not of love, but from dependency. The maturing human being must now take initiatives toward human strangers, initiatives of the touches of friendship and sexual love.

Those having been well-touched take to love naturally; those who never or seldom felt the warm sympathy of touch in their childhood find love difficult to learn. But even for those latter, late touches can humanize and teach love. We never outgrow our need for the sympathy of the contact of body to body.

Coitus is the highest creativity of loving touch. For coitus is not an assault or a grappling, but the most intense and personally concentrated other-affirming human touch. All of our aware-ness—of ourselves, of others, of our humanness, even of our participation in the great current of Life—culminates in that utmost intimacy. At that moment, we touch Life Itself.

As I have so often chanted in refrain, the phys-ical is the way to the spiritual. So, the touch is sacramental. It can sanctify. Do not touch each other with indifference.

The tactile tenderness of one person toward another is the most simple, but one of the most sublime experiences we can have in life.

313

This world of straight lines and sharp angles and hard surfaces,—how desensitizing is the technosphere that is our environment.

Impermeable artificiality all around, when a man reaches out to touch, there are only the cold inert surfaces of his own creations, the ever-increasing complex of our manufactures. What good is it all to the organic human being?

Clothed, wrapped up, I reach out in all directions. Everything I touch is synthetic, fabricated, the myriad of contrived things with which we have surrounded ourselves.

Man amongst his machines and devices, pushing himself against his own contrivances. We are rich in the things that have impoverished our organic vitality. We have ostracized Nature and erected urban utopia in its stead. We have made our world hard.

We attempt to harden our bodies too, so that we as individuals may function in our functioning technology, automatons in an automonotonous world.

What has this technosphere done to us? How we chatter at each other like electronic media, how we cold-function like the machines and devices!

No, my love, this world is not for us. Come, take my hand, remember the human animal we once were. Shed your clothes, as I will shed mine. Relax and soften to me, as I will soften to you. Naked each, let us remember and recover ourselves and each other. Draw near, your living warmth to mine.

Awkward, yes we are awkward in attempting the natural, especially in a first encounter. Perhaps we are even afraid. Afraid of nakedness. You still are dressed in your civilized compunctions and propriety; you cover yourself in shame.

Do not be afraid or ashamed. Try to remember the good memory, back in the early days of our race, our own earlier life, that warm, glowing animality that is of the essence of what we are.

Come, my love, draw nearer, my love, surrender to our human relatedness to each other.

Ah, yes...this soft, wet warm intermingling. You and I, male and female, regaining touch with our essential nature.

Why fear naked togetherness with another? All around us are those straight lines and sharp angles and hard surfaces. You and I have escaped the technological environment to return to Nature. We rediscover our authentic being. We are vibrant, animate, passionate, attracting and attractive lovers and mates.

314

Solitude is the necessary prelude to intimacy.

In this modern world of the masses, we rub against one another too much, dulling our awareness, blunting out sensitivity.

Numbers is the enemy of sensuousness. After the crowds have knocked us around a few times, we learn to keep our distance one from another. Anonymous, indiscriminate bumping intrudes upon our individual integrity. We deal with it by gradually encasing our skin in a hide.

The many bodies around us, all blurring by, overwhelm our senses. To protect ourselves from sensory injury, we contract, like the worm that has been stepped on, to use Nietzsche's simile.

In the chronic tension of the tight-packed urban crowds, sex can become a hostile pushing-back, a retaliation, an assertive attempt to escape impersonality. That kind of sex is a punch and counter-punch. The contagion of crowds is aggression.

Let each of us steal away alone, then, and strip naked in utter silence and serene solitude. Some places in our crowded world still exist where this can be done.

Bathe. Rest. Recover. Become cleaned and calmed. Let all others and all the world be kept at a distance for a while. Rediscover the wholesomeness of your own body and the value of your separate soul.

That is the necessary restorative therapy, the convalescence that every modern person needs before seeking the experience of intimacy.

When we are naked and alone, we do not wear our warmth, we generate it from within. No longer bombarded by sexual propaganda, we feel instead stirrings rising naturally from within, rhythmically attuned to the flow of blood, the beating of the heart, the rise and fall of respiration.

Alone and restored, I love my living body and myself. Then, at leisure, in self-possessed calm, without any compulsion, in spontaneity, I will love my woman.

I have been alone and there rediscovered myself as a male and as a man. Escaping the crowd, I recovered my individuality...and my incompleteness. I am whole, but I am aware of my halfness.

So now I need my woman. I am refreshed, ready to offer myself. I have been alone. Now I can love.

315

Perhaps I have been alone too much. Do you sense that? Is that why you have sought me out to be with me today?

Have I become woebegone and forlorn in my vocational discipline of solitude? Too much stewing in my own juices for my own good?

You come to me and smile and take my hand. I am embarrassed, I feel ashamed. How can I receive the gift of yourself? I am not worthy of you.

You look into my eyes, into my soul. You brush away my worst as just so much accumulated dust. You insist that I *am* worthy; you insist on seeing me better than I have ever dreamt I could be.

You understand my loneliness and my privation. You are willing to risk even yourself in your belief in the man I am becoming. You let yourself go, you let your self go. You trust me, you love me, you believe in me.

I cannot be bad in your presence. Your eyes are the mirror of my best self. When I look at you looking at me, I see the best that I can be. Lover, my life, keeper-of-faith!

There are sex-seekers who use the one they find. And others who find acceptance in sex. But you are not just for yourself and are not driven by need. Your yielding of self in sex is an act of faith and an affirmation of both of us.

You have found me in my aloneness and abandoned yourself into our togetherness. You yield, and I must yield, to you, to my best self, to the two of us becoming one.

316

There is no complete man without woman, nor complete woman without man.

The other sex must sexualize our sexuality.

317

I look upon the naked human body with the elation of desire and the melancholy of compassion. Nothing is more attractive to me, yet nothing is more philosophically disheartening. The naked body is a parable of all human love and loss.

Pornography cannot disfigure wholesome corporal integrity. The body of a woman is something more beautiful than art has ever depicted. How I love and long for the body of woman!

If Christian scruple would close my eyes and turn me away, I would set up within myself the torturing tension of resistance to the most sublime aesthetic vision a man may have. At the same time, I would shun the most truthful image of the poignance of our human lives.

The naked body of a woman...exposed, open, vulnerable. Even in the insistence of my desire, I perceive her vulnerability and her mortality.

Body beautiful, body mortal, I long for you, I love you. But when I reach out to touch you, I feel the tragic temporality of human sex and love.

Your body, like my own, is a process-in-time, ever advancing toward destined extinction. The human body is a shooting star of Life's self-image, blazing and soaring, but quickly expending itself, burning up, burning out.

My body and the body of the one I love are symbols of our human tragedy. We are together as I write this, but a time will come when we will both be gone. We are flames dreading and anticipating the inevitable day of our snuffing-out. Extinguishable, mortal, ephemeral...doomed.

My yearning for the naked body is a lust for Life. But an ache mingles with my desire. Our *joy wants eternity*, even as we know that both our wanting and our joy are mortal. Next to the immediacy of sex lies the imminence of death. Death is the third intimate in every conjugal bed.

I clasp the naked body of my beloved to me. I embrace her...and myself, our life...and our death.

318

The body of a woman is a vessel containing all the mysteries of Life. The soul of a woman is a repository for all the organic wisdom of Nature. If a man is to live, if he is to learn anything, he must seek ultimate enlightenment in the body and soul of a woman.

The womb and female desire are the cosmic mechanism and dynamism in miniature. Every woman I meet is a symbol; every feminine acquaintance I make is a revelation. Femaleness itself is a profound, indeed an unfathomable miracle.

I look at a woman with passion and wonder. Who would not tremble at the attempt to seduce the embodiment of all Life and Nature?

I yearn to embrace her, to know her, to know the All in her. Sex and love are stages in my ascent toward understanding. I have guessed at woman's deep secret. Now I aspire to achieve by emulative willpower what she accomplishes by simply being. But God has forbidden man to desire woman; the patriarchal God is jealous of the body and soul of woman.

Woman is the riddle, and woman is the answer to the riddle. What she does not reveal she nonetheless knows by intuition and instinct.

When a woman is present, the black universe is flooded with the light of meaning. Wondrous, mysterious woman. The secret of Life stands naked before me:—

319

There is something deeply comforting in the sight of a woman's bosom, that soft and sensual suspension. They are warm and soothing, those breasts of flesh and fat and blood and milk. And beneath is the beat of the heart, lapping the face of the lover in its liquid rhythm. A man presses his cheek into the yielding undular mass, and all the sharp edges of the world are smoothed. Smoothed, soothed.

320

I feel the lure-of-the-lower, whenever I look at the undulating, fleshy billows of the female torso. The force of libidinal gravity draws my gaze down past the breasts and into the swirling deep currents of the lower belly and the confluence of flesh waves, those crests and crevices, that flow into the maelstrom.

It is a sea-fever I feel, because the bottomless well, the visceral Deep, of a woman is an oceanic cosmos into which I long to plunge. My desire is a surge of salty seed toward the saline-sea of the womb. The abyss of a female body is nothing less than a microcosm of the primordial amniotic ocean from which all life emerged at the birth of evolution..."And I long to go down to the sea again."

Yes, my lust is a longing to go down, to go into her, to go back to Life. Male sexual desire is a nostalgia, a yearning to suspend oneself and float senseless and unconscious in the Ocean of Origin, to drown oneself in the maternal Sea, to expend one's life where it was engendered. Instinct is atavistic; it is a powerful retrogressive force impelling the male to die himself back into Life.

The curves of the lower female body, which swell, peak, then recede as she moves—that alluring tidal tension of the skin—,—how it draws me down to the sea within her!

The naked female body is Life Itself exposed. I reach out and touch the hot skin, which is moist from the vaporous transpiration rising out of the seething salt-sea. And, at my touch, she brims and boils.

My rage to plunge intensifies as the hot, swirling streams of her body lap me with fiery salt-tongues. I am afloat and adrift on the surface of her body, a burning ember soaking itself in a flaming sea. I descend in a blind groping toward the Avernus of Life's liquid conflagration. Down... past the navel, sealed entrance into the fetal bowels, shriveled line of the life that first flowed into her from the womb-ocean of her mother. Down...Down...

Tossed in the tempest, incandescently burning, I glide eagerly into the gulf, where the base of her body and the portal to the Deep swell convulsively.

And there beneath the foam and spray is the vortex of the whirlpool swirling down into the Sea of Life itself.

I plunge myself, to consume her and be swallowed up by her, to lose my self and her self in the selflessness of sensations.

An upsurge of salty froth lubricates my descent, as I plummet—life-mad!—into the conical well of the boiling water-womb. I submerge myself completely, I drown in delirium. Life, I die for thee!

But the Sea of Life is unfathomable. The mystery of Life, and of woman, vessel of life, is impenetrable. After having fecundated her, I bob to the surface again, buoyant now that I am emptied. The male is a hollow stick that the sea forces upward, tosses about among the waves, and, at last, carries along in tide to dry and wither on some sandy shore. And so, I am cast off, from her and from Life, I just driftwood, a dead and dry piece of the land that does not belong in the living aqueous ambience of the Sea.

That is the poignance and pathos of the male, who, after responding to the siren call of Life, is used for a brief service, then discarded. I sense how I, as a male, must always be apart from the essence of Life, deprived of the bliss of eternal immersion in it.

When I look at the sea-swells of a woman's lower body, when I feel a deep longing for her, I know that I can, but only episodically, drown myself in Life. And that is the mystical meaning of the biological act. Coitus is life-immersion, for the man who descends into Life, and for the woman who envelops the body and seed of her lover to engender new life. Can anything we ever do as human beings be more sacred than that?

321

Body of man, animate earth,
Corporal continent and volatile volcano—
Mountainous, muscular, masterful—
Heats and hardens in peninsular promontory
And, extension extending, extends itself:—
Body of man, mystery of man!

Body of woman, animate sea,
Oral ocean and all-accepting amnion—
Fluvial and flowing, billowing, boiling—
Opens absorbing and ardent,
Engulfs and laps and loves her lover:—
Body of woman, mystery of woman!

Bodies of both, animate mingling,
Earth in an amnion, body in body—
Volcanic and tidal in fiery fusion—
Enact the explosion of primordial birth;
Absorption absorbing extension extended:—
Mystery of mingling, mystery of Life!

322

The most transcendent encounter a man may experience in life is the frantic, clinging embrace of a woman burning in the delirium of incandescence. The apogee of ecstatic intimacy with the All is within that moment of explosive fusion:—the utter nakedness of naked intermingling!

323

Our bodies aflame and fluid, pores dilated and oozing out their brine. The mouth awash, ears full, nose aroused, eyes expansive, the brain twisted to tight intensity. Pulse arace, heartbeat hammering, temples coursing in rapid throbs. Tumescence and the heavy, heavy bloat of thick blood.

Total touch of the two bodies. Then the easy tender slide of entry. The depths of the boiling cauldron and liquid flames from the viscera. Rocking convulsions, furious rhythms, and gasping, gasping for breath, for life!

Then the rise of geyser jets of feeling and pleasure and intense, all-overcoming sensations. Climax, crisis, crescendo! An electric instant of cosmic convergence. The death in life!

Some spasms and ebb, and the slow, steady flow down from the peak through furrows to quiet valleys. Lapsing, receding, falling...down, back down to the temperate temperatures again.

But the lingering pleasure and pain. The swoon, the sleepiness, faint, faint. Unconsciousness. Blackout. . .and dreams.

324

Afterglow. Aftermath.

We are intimate even during her unconsciousness:

By my side she lies, the moist warmth of her face pressed to my shoulder, her hair tingling the exposed length of my bare arm, her limbs entwined around me in the tender laxity of sleep. The two of us are in the elemental animal togetherness.

I place my hand upon her neck and feel the undulant life-throbs, which are echoed and reverberated in a synchronous pulse in my own fingertips.

Now and then she sighs, anxious in her dreaming, awakens in her touch, clings closer to me, then, secure, sleeps on with steady breathing. Even in her sleep, she assents to me, affirms me, reaches out for my strength, child to her father, sister to her brother, lover to her mate.

My body weighs down into the swallowing softness of the bed and is absorbed into the soft fleshiness of the woman beside me. An aura of radiant warmth and animal aroma. The two of us bundled together, lulled in the cradle of a childlike embrace.

325

We inhale another, exhale ourselves, pulsate and pause between pulses to perceive the pulses of the other. The silence between my heartbeats is filled by her heartbeats between my silences, as, in antiphon, we pound out the eversounding throb...the hot, liquid pounding, the steady beat of life's dynamic.

326

The means to psychological health that I would prescribe may be summarized in one short, simple word,—sex.

I mean, of course, not plural acts, but a singular mated relatedness.

327

Two want to be one.

Within the body of the male, suspended in symmetry, the two globes teeming with gametes wriggling in restlessness to flow forward in freshet through the fluid lifeline:—Two want to be one.

Within the body of the female, suspended in symmetry, the two globes teeming with gametes, one of which buds and bursts forth and flows down through the conduit seeking:—Two want to be one.

The bodies of the male and female, pulling each other to earth, interpenetrating, surging, submerging, flowing together, each into the other:—Two want to be one.

Then, impregnation, the zygote, fracture of one cell split into two. From that very instant:—Two want to be one.

328

The intercourse between bodies is a prelude to the microcosmic coitus of conception. A man and a woman having exhausted themselves and each other, the teeming gametes surge ahead, ovum descending, sperm ascending, to perform a second intercourse, that one with all the passion of Life Itself.

Only after the man and woman have tired of their sex and fallen from each other does conception occur. The spermatozoon seconds his master's effort and consummates the act of life upon the mistress's miniature. With the penetration of the ovum, the male's immersion in the female body is achieved at last, the fusion of the sexes complete.

Men and women are only escorts for germinal paramours, and receive their wages in pleasure. Then the woman's body becomes the warm, wet bed in which the ultimate sex-act is effected, that between the unseen homunculus and the feminuncula. . .

She is sleeping by my side, as I smile about these musings. I should wake her up and ask permission to use a speculum and spyglass with which I could peep in on Nature's most passionate performance.

329

Sex as a pleasure...If only it were so simple.

No, sex is not merely pleasurable, nor is it simple. There *is* gratification in sex, one so intense that it may be excruciatingly painful. But that pleasure wedded to pain puts one into intimacy with death, as it does with Life. How terrible, then, is that encounter, how intimidating the experience! I approach prospects to intimacy with anxiety.

The helpless abandonment of oneself to imperious drive, the starkness of physical and psychological nakedness, the overwhelming pain of the pleasure, the metaphysical swoon of the aftermath, the gradual return to clearheaded consciousness, the awareness of what was done, the loss of self and the intense intimacy with the other:—How awesome is it all. Sex is dreadful, awful in the act and in the insights.

I approach a woman with tremulous compulsion. I have lost all control and presence of self. My body throbs with the insistence of primordial instinct. I am attracted and inhibited, paralyzed and driven forward at the same time.

We draw to each other, naked, tense. What has been within us now comes over us, overcomes us, compels us to its own purpose. From tentative touch to clutching embrace to total intermingling, we fall into momentary loss of both consciousness and separate individuality.

Shouldn't we cry out in fright at what happens in coitus? With the revelatory awareness of the inevitable eventual loss of our lives, how terrible, how tragic is the experience of the keenest intensity that Life offers. The plot of that tragedy is laid out before us, sand, at that, the psychologists and pornographers fixate on the pleasure we receive.

What is any brief episodic gratification, compared to all the grim implications? Sexual relations,—self-indulgence, mere time-killing distraction and diversion? No. Sexual intercourse is stark confrontation with the truth of our frailty and mortality.

Who has the courage for such realization? Who has the courage to lose his life in another and return to oneself with a deepened awareness of death?

Pleasure? Terror!

330

The night before last, I suffered a nightmare in which Death, as a coffin enshrouded in a white bedsheet, hovered over me, while I lay prostrate in terror.

There was an epic quality to the dream-scene; it was staged in a manner like the portrayals of confrontation with the metaphysical that I see every day in the religious art of Rome.

I awoke, trembling, blinking in the darkness, and struggling to regain hold of my conscious self.

I pondered the dream yesterday and anticipated a rematch, as it were. Hence, cowardice!

And so, last night I dreamt of being harassed by a squad of devils. At first, I tried to drive them off by holding a small crucifix and extending the martyred body toward them in an attempted exorcism. The devils were intrigued, but not frightened off by the idol. I ran about frantically waving the crucifix, in an effort to herd the demons to a cliff, where Christ and I would dispose of them.

The symbol of conquest of death through undergoing agonizing death followed by resurrection was availing me little against my adversaries.

But then I saw that one of the devils was a woman who was Death. Throwing aside the crucifix, I leapt with lust upon her, fearlessly embracing her seductive, yielding body.

At that, the other devils, out of modesty, withdrew.

The shroudy vestments of the she-devil were bedsheets that I cast aside in my passion. Devil-Death-Woman, I lust for you!

I awoke from the dream in the dark early morning, throbbing on the verge of conquering consummation. This time the nightmare had fled from me and not I from the nightmare. Death is a squeamish virgin. She plays the harlot, but let her barely glimpse the male staff-of-life and she vanishes in maidenly fright.

You cannot deal Death a dose of death, so the crucified god is an ambitious pretender in the realm of Death. Yet, lust-love-Life sends all the devils scurrying over the cliffs.

My dreams are parables told to me by a wise unconscious.

As I lay awake in the moment after the climax—or, should I say, after the climax that eluded me—I smiled in satisfaction. Perhaps tonight I will lurk in ambush for She-Death and success- fully effect the ravishment at last.

331

The only triumph over death, momentary and illusory though it is, is coitus, the sacramental celebration of Life. The intensity of aliveness at orgasm banishes for those few moments all consciousness of self, and, therefore, of death and awareness of death.

Instinct and Life triumph against mortality and inevitability.

332

Today I am going to remain within the confines of my room in the *pensione*, all day, except for brief absences for my necessary meals. The Spartan furnishings of my room are a relaxation to my eyes and mind. Too much pagan art, too much naked sculpture, has left me overstimulated and frazzled.

My senses and my sensitivity need a respite and recuperation. So, I'll hole up this dull, drizzly Roman day. I'll spend a whole day of my life looking at plain white walls and ceiling, calming down and clearing my mind.

What have I learned from my odyssey among the islands of Mediterranean pagan imagination, anyway? When I looked at all those idols, what did I see? Visions, or mere hallucinations? Did Hermaphrodite seduce me into the innermost realm of instinct or only down some byways of fantasy? When I started out, I knew only what the male knows, and that is not very much. What have I learned since? Am I only back where I started from?

Well, when we go off on an excursion, we do hope to get somewhere. I may have wandered into aimlessness, gotten hopelessly lost, and found my way home only by blind luck. Suitably chastened, I'll undertake no outside excursion today. I've got to figure out where to venture next.

So that this day of self-imposed confinement is not completely unproductive, I'll write out one last rumination on instinct, one that may provide a bridge to a new theme:—

* * *

The female feels an instinctive guardedness a-gainst trespass upon her body.

And so, women stop shyly when faced with the sexual intensity of their men. They are reluctant to descend into indulgence in gross carnal sensuality. Men, of course, try to pressure women over the brink. That interplay of female resistance and male insistence has created a chronic tension in the relationship between the sexes (not to mention the constant motif in the plots of many Romantic novels).

Whether a woman yields, only to recoil in old-fashioned guilt or in second-guessing regret of bad judgment, or whether she steadfastly denies herself sex and thus frigidifies, both her doing and her not-doing become repugnant to her and to the man. Then does the relationship between the sexes deteriorate into resentful or hostile estrangement.

The Romantics presented women as so spiritualized by culture that they could engage in sex only through a condescension or an outright self-debasement. Women wanted love of course, but did they have sexual desires at all?

Women are as fully motivated by erotic need as are men, so psychoanalysis and feminism now tell us. The sexes share an interest in mutual self-gratification, we are assured. Psychoanalysis gave women the dispensation. Feminism now gives them the license.

But if women are by constitution as animally amorous as men, we ask, "Why reluctant?" Why do women still hesitate from satisfying their own deepest instinctual needs? Men leap to every opportunity to sexual adventure; they are only being true to their own nature. Why are women cautious? How is their self-control to be explained?

That civilization's code of repression incapacitated women from expressing spontaneous sexuality was true in earlier societies—Dr. Freud's diagnosis—, but our *liberated* contemporary woman suffers no imposed restraint. Liberated though women are, they do not use their freedom to indiscriminately dispense their favors to all the pleading men. Healthy women still hold themselves back.

Such former deterrents as fear of pregnancy or venereal disease have lost their force through modern contraceptives and antibiotics. The cult of chastity is no longer held in high repute. Even the commandment against fornication is a dead letter.

The reason that the healthy woman is not promiscuous, despite her license to be so, is an instinctual and psychological one, what I would call *woman's deep secret*. That secret is both the explanation for female abstinence and the prescription for full female participation in sexual surrender.

Woman's deep secret is love.

It is not because female sexuality is a weak and wishy-washy drive that women appear inhibited and uninterested in sex. Rather, it is because their drive is so deep, so intense, so permeating, that they must protect themselves from it by abstinence, until they receive an assurance and commitment, namely, that they are loved.

Only then will they willingly plunge into an animal fervor and carnality of such power that, by comparison, male drive seems a small-and-sometimes thing.

Because of the intensity of their feelings, women are vulnerable, and they realize it. If a woman doesn't protect herself, she is likely to be used and discarded. Women truly suffer more in their love life than do men. Instinctual wisdom directs a woman to withhold herself until she is sure of being loved. The man must bring to her a commitment to match her own involvement of the whole person in erotic relatedness.

Then, the woman loved is the eager lover. In a woman's soul, love is arousal. A truly aroused woman exudes more burning, intense, carnal passion than a man could ever exhaust.

Is she reluctant, hesitant? If you want her, man, you must learn woman's deep secret. Learn love. Then, look out! She will make it seem to you as if the cosmos itself is afire.

I have long been convinced—(by life-experience, not by those psychology textbooks that I tossed out before my very first excursion into instinct)—, I have been convinced, I say, of the absolute superiority of female instinct to male mere drive. Woman is thoroughly sexualized through all her being, whereas man seems sexualized only in his doings.

Men must painstakingly acquire what comes so naturally to women, that is, a personalization of general instinct, in short, a fully committed mating choice.

Women know what the supreme human sexual experience is,—the fusion of organic instinct into conscious personal choice, of passion into compassion, of lust into love. Woman says to man, "Because I love you, I make love to you. This is for you, as I am for you." Sex then enters into the soul; Eros and Psyche give each other a tender kiss.

The solution to the human problem of sex is to be found neither in repressive morality nor in psychoanalytic therapy. It is to be found in a woman's good instinct. Men must learn what women already know. Men must learn love.

END

Instinct

Roman Ruminations, Volume Two

About **Roman Ruminations**

Roman Ruminations presents "the psychology of the human as enculturated animal". If the human is a cultural creature, what better setting for consideration could there be than Rome, The Cosmopolis, one place on earth that contains the all of culture?

In Rome, you learn by venturing out on itineraries. *Roman Ruminations*, then, is a walking tour through human psychology in culture. *Loneliness* is treated within the contexts of literature and music, *Instinct* the contexts of mythology and classical sculpture, and *Love* in the contexts of religion, philosophy, education and art. The human mind is revealed by those activities and products of human culture.

The *Roman Ruminations* trilogy is not a quick-and-easy 1-2-3. Roman itineraries seem random and sometimes wayward—are we getting anywhere?—, but just around the next corner there might be the very insight we are seeking. We know that we won't solve the human or fully understand. Even so, there will be some revelations along our Roman way. Insight is expressed in the "Aha!" of an aphorism.

The characteristic Roman craft was mosaic, lots of little pieces put together to make a picture. *Roman Ruminations* is a literary mosaic, five hundred little pieces from which, for those who stand far back enough, a picture may emerge. *Roman Ruminations* is a mosaic of the mind.

Roman Ruminations
>   Volume One, *Loneliness* (sections 1-164)
>   Volume Two, *Instinct* (sections 165-332)
>   Volume Three, *Love* (sections 333-500)

Roman Ruminations (Complete) and each volume separately are all available as eBooks or paperbacks.